YOUNG STUDENTS

Learning Library

VOLUME 9

Fraction–Growth

WEEKLY READER BOOKS
MIDDLETOWN·CONNECTICUT

PHOTO CREDITS

CONTENTS

FRACTION We all take fractions for granted. We know that if we cut an apple in half we have two equal parts, called "halves." But it was not so easy for the ancient Egyptians. Before they invented fractions, how did they find the answer to 3 divided by 2? After a time a clever Egyptian invented a symbol that meant "a part of." People used this symbol when writing a fraction of a whole number.

Later, about 900 years ago, a Hindu astrologer, Bhaskara, invented a new way of writing fractions. We call fractions written this way *common fractions*. ¼ is a common fraction. A pie divided into 4 equal parts produces 4 quarters. Each is ¼ of the pie.

In a common fraction the number above the line is the *numerator*. The number below the line is the *denominator*.

Decimal fractions, invented by the Belgian-Dutch mathematician Simon Stevinus about 1600, are used even more than common fractions—in money, for example. We don't write: "$1¼"! We write: "$1.25." We use decimals a lot because they are much easier to work with.

ALSO READ: DECIMAL NUMBER, METRIC SYSTEM, NUMBER.

FRACTURE A fracture is a broken bone. A very hard blow or too sharp a bend can cause a fracture. Sometimes even just a sharp cough can break a rib. Anyone—young or old—can break a bone, but old people are more likely to suffer fractures, because their bones are much more fragile.

There are several kinds of fractures. If a bone breaks in only one place and does not poke through the skin surrounding the break, this is a

◀ *Mont St. Michel, off the coast of northern Brittany, France. At low tide you can walk across to it.* (See France)

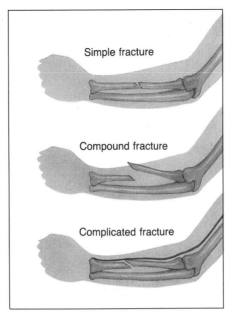

▲ *Simple fractures are painful but usually not serious. In a compound fracture the skin is pierced by the bone. In a complicated fracture, a blood vessel might be injured.*

simple fracture. In a *compound*, or *open*, fracture, the skin is pierced by the ends of the bone. A compound fracture is more serious than a simple fracture because it is open to germs and because it damages tissues. When the bone breaks in more than one place, it is called a *multiple* fracture. In a *comminuted* fracture a bone shatters into many pieces. In a *greenstick* fracture a bone cracks but does not break.

A broken bone tends to heal by itself. Tissues grow out from the broken ends. The tissues eventually grow together and form a solid connection. If the broken ends are not in their natural position, they join in a deformed manner. So a doctor *sets* the pieces (moves them into their natural positions), and holds the broken pieces in place with a splint or cast.

If you think that someone has a fracture of a major bone, such as a leg or an arm, do not let the person move. Call a doctor immediately.

ALSO READ: BONE, FIRST AID, SKELETON.

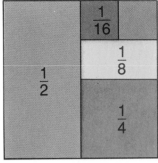

▲ *This square has been divided into smaller areas. These are fractions of the original area. How many times can you fit the area marked "¹/₁₆" into the area marked "¹/₂"?*

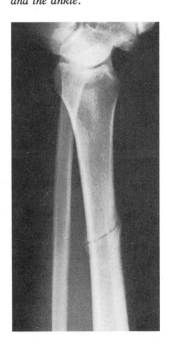

▼ *An X ray of a simple fracture of the tibia, or shinbone, the long bone between the knee and the ankle.*

▲ *The Eiffel Tower is one of the great landmarks of Paris, the capital of France.*

FRANCE France is a beautiful and pleasant country famous for its rich cultural life. France's cooking, delicious cheeses, and fine wines are enjoyed the world over. Women who can afford it come from all over the world to buy clothes from the dress designers of Paris. French writers have created some of the world's greatest literature and poetry. The country's artists, especially its modern painters and sculptors, are also famous. Many famous composers have been French.

France is the largest country in western Europe. The high mountains called the Pyrenees form France's border with Spain in the South. The Jura Mountains and the snow-covered French Alps in the east separate it from Switzerland and Italy. France's west coast is on the Atlantic Ocean. France also has a coast to the southeast on the Mediterranean Sea, dotted with lovely resorts. The Mediterranean island of Corsica is also a part of France. The nation's capital is Paris, located on the north side of the

▲ *A field of lavender bushes in Provence, in southeast France.*

Seine River. Paris was founded in the 3rd century B.C. and became the capital of France in A.D. 987.

France has a variety of climates. The northern part of the country is warmer than might be expected so far north. Warm, moist winds come from the ocean, making winters mild. In the eastern part of the country, the Alps get much snow in the winter, making them an excellent place to ski. The southern part of France has warm, moist winters and hot, sunny summers.

The great variety in climate and the fertile soil make France a rich agricultural country. Farmers grow wheat, fruits, and vegetables in the north and west. Olive trees and wine grapes grow in the warm southern section.

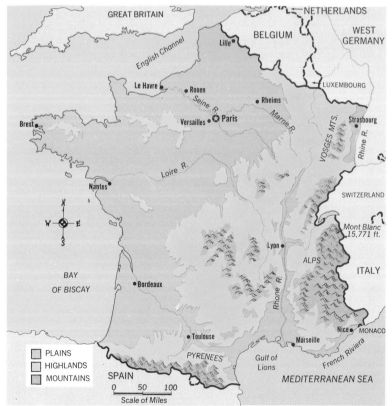

PLAINS
HIGHLANDS
MOUNTAINS

FRANCE

Capital City: Paris (2,166,000 people).
Area: 211,208 square miles (547,026 sq. km).
Population: 55,000,000.
Government: Republic.
Natural Resources: Iron ore, bauxite, potash, lumber.
Export Products: Machinery, transportation equipment, chemicals, iron and steel, textiles, wine, cereal grains.
Unit of Money: Franc.
Official Language: French.

France is also an industrial country. Leading industrial products are textiles, metal products, automobiles, and chemicals. The iron mines of Lorraine in eastern France are among the richest in the world.

France is one of the oldest European nations. Charlemagne, who ruled the land in the 800's, was one of the country's greatest kings. Other kings ruled France until the French Revolution that lasted from 1789 to 1799. The nobility lost power, and the common people gained new rights. France dominated Europe during the Napoleonic era in the early 1800's.

Prussian (German) armies invaded France during the Franco-Prussian War from 1870 to 1871. Germans again invaded the country in World War I and World War II. These wars caused much bitterness between France and Germany. France's prestige in world affairs was restored under the leadership of Charles de Gaulle from 1958 to 1969. Under de Gaulle, France became a founder-member of the European Community, with a strong economy and independent foreign policy. Its relations with Germany became friendly. Leaders after de Gaulle continued to encourage an independent French role in world affairs.

ALSO READ: CHARLEMAGNE; DE GAULLE, CHARLES; FRENCH HISTORY; FRENCH REVOLUTION; NAPOLEON BONAPARTE; PARIS.

France has almost no oil reserves. Therefore, nuclear power is very important. About 40 percent of all the country's electricity supply comes from nuclear power.

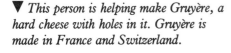

▼ *This person is helping make Gruyère, a hard cheese with holes in it. Gruyère is made in France and Switzerland.*

▼ *France's TGV is world-famous. "TGV" stands for "Train à Grande Vitesse," French for "high-speed train."*

▲ *King Francis I of France. He spent most of his reign fighting with Holy Roman Emperor Charles V. Francis believed that he, not Charles, should be Holy Roman Emperor.*

▼ *St. Francis of Assisi was a friend to all the animals as well as his fellow human beings.*

FRANCIS, KINGS OF FRANCE

Two kings of France were called Francis.

Francis I (1494–1547) was a ruler who fought wars. He became king in 1515 and soon set out to take back land in Italy that France had once ruled. He won the Battle of Marignano (1515) and conquered part of Italy. His great rival was Charles V, the Holy Roman Emperor. Francis believed that he, not Charles, should have this crown. He fought against Charles for many years. He tried to get Henry VIII of England to join his fight, but Henry refused. Francis lost the Battle of Pavia in Italy in 1525 and was taken prisoner. He promised to give up the French lands of Flanders, Artois, and Burgundy, in addition to all the land in Italy taken by France, in return for his freedom. Francis and Charles fought each other two more times. When the first war ended, Burgundy became French territory again. However, Francis did not get Flanders and Artois back.

Francis I had a love for the arts. He hired architects to build castles (*châteaux*) in the Loire valley of France. He had many writers and artists at his court—including Leonardo da Vinci. Portraits were painted of him that show him as a cunning and powerful monarch.

Francis II (1544–1560) was the grandson of Francis I. He reigned for only 17 months. His uncles ran France while he was king. In 1558, he married Mary Stuart, who later became Mary, Queen of Scots. He was only 16 when he died.

ALSO READ: CHARLES, HOLY ROMAN EMPERORS; FRENCH HISTORY; MARY, QUEEN OF SCOTS.

FRANCIS OF ASSISI (about 1182–1226)

Francis of Assisi, known for his gentleness and kindness, is one of the greatest saints.

Francis was the son of a wealthy merchant of Assisi, Italy. As a young man, he enjoyed a life of gaiety and pleasure. He became a soldier at age 20 and fought in a war between the Italian city-states of Assisi and Perugia. He was taken prisoner by the Perugians, and during his captivity developed a serious illness.

During his illness, Francis heard voices telling him to give up all his possessions and preach the teachings of Jesus. Although his father was furious, Francis obeyed the voices. He traveled barefoot in tattered clothes as far as Egypt and Palestine. He carried no money, and had to rely on the kindness of the people along his way. He became known for his kindness to animals. He once preached to a flock of birds about the love of God.

People began to follow Francis and accept his teachings. He started the Franciscan order of the Roman Catholic Church. A young girl from Assisi, later called Saint Clare, joined his followers. Francis founded a Franciscan order of nuns, the "Poor Clares," for her. Many orders of Franciscan monks and nuns still continue his work.

In later life, strange marks appeared on Francis's body. These *stigmata* resembled the wounds Christ received when crucified. Francis spent his last years in pain—but he continued to pray and preach. He was buried in a small church in Assisi.

In 1228, Francis was declared a saint by Pope Gregory IX. His feast day is October 4.

ALSO READ: SAINT.

FRANCO, FRANCISCO (1892–1975)

Francisco Franco was fascist dictator of Spain for more than 30 years. Franco graduated from a military academy, and then went into the Spanish army. He was made a general at age 32.

Civil war began in Spain in 1936.

Franco became the leader of the rebels. His army defeated the *Loyalists* (supporters of the Spanish government) in 1939, and Franco named himself the new head of the Spanish government and army. He also controlled the fascist political party, the Falange. No other political parties were permitted in Spain.

Franco kept power in Spain by controlling the army, the police, and the newspapers. He worked closely with wealthy Spanish factory owners and businessmen, and they helped him keep control of the country. He was also on good terms with the Roman Catholic Church. This was important because nearly all Spaniards are Catholic.

During World War II, Franco said that Spain was *neutral* (not involved in the war). He did send troops to help Germany fight the Soviet Union. But when he saw that Germany would lose the war, he ordered the troops back and again said that Spain was neutral.

In 1969, Franco named Prince Juan Carlos of Bourbon as his successor. Juan Carlos, the grandson of the last king of Spain before Franco, became king and head of state when Franco died in 1975.

ALSO READ: FASCISM, SPAIN, SPANISH HISTORY, WORLD WAR II.

FRANKLIN, BENJAMIN (1706–1790) Benjamin Franklin is often called North America's first great man. He succeeded in many fields. He was a printer, businessman, author, scientist, inventor, philosopher, ambassador, and statesman.

Franklin was born to a poor Puritan family in Boston, Massachusetts, 70 years before the birth of the United States, in which he played such an important role. He was the fifteenth child in a family of 17 children. He went to school for only two years, but he educated himself by reading and studying many books.

Franklin went to work for an older brother, James, a printer, at the age of 12. When James was thrown in jail for criticizing Massachusetts officials, young Benjamin wrote and printed their paper, the *New England Courant*, one of the first newspapers in North America. When James later lost his license to continue the newspaper, Ben secretly became the publisher. But life with his brother was not easy, so Benjamin ran away at age 17. He went to New York, but could not find a job. He then went to Philadelphia where he was employed in a print shop.

Franklin eventually started his own print shop, and then bought his own newspaper, the *Pennsylvania Gazette*, in 1729. He formed partnerships with other printers to start newspapers and printing shops in other parts of the colonies as well. He began publishing *Poor Richard's Almanack* in the 1730's. It contained practical and witty sayings that made him famous—"He that riseth late must trot all day," "Fish and visitors stink after three days."

Franklin became increasingly involved in public life. He helped to start the first library in the colonies (the American Philosophical Society) and the Academy of Philadelphia, which later became the University of Pennsylvania. He organized Philadelphia's first fire department, improved the city's street paving and lighting, and raised money for the first city hospital. He served as the Clerk of the Pennsylvania Assembly, as well as Postmaster of Philadelphia. He later became deputy Postmaster General of all the colonies.

Franklin was always interested in science, and he made many contributions to the science of electricity. Best known is his kite-flying experiment. He tied a metal key to the metal wire of a kite which he flew during a thunderstorm. Lightning hit the wire, and a spark of electricity flashed

▲ *Francisco Franco, dictator of Spain from 1939 until his death in 1975. Since 1975 Spain has been a democracy.*

▲ *Benjamin Franklin, great American scientist, statesman, writer, and wit.*

▲ *Benjamin Franklin showed that lightning was electrical by flying a kite during a thunderstorm, and drawing sparks from a metal key tied to the lower end of the string. Several people died trying to do this experiment. Franklin was very lucky!*

Along with his other activities, Benjamin Franklin wrote his *Autobiography*. Not only does it give important information to historians, but it is fun and easy to read.

out of the key, proving that lightning was a form of electricity. (This experiment can be very dangerous and is likely to kill you. Do not try it yourself!) Franklin also reasoned that electricity could flow along a conductor such as a wire. He was the first person to use many electrical terms still used today, such as "positive," "negative," "battery," and "conductor." He was interested in other scientific subjects as well, including physics, chemistry, meteorology (the study of weather), and oceanography (the study of oceans and seas). He invented the Franklin stove, which used less fuel than a fireplace. The Franklin stove is still manufactured. He also developed the lightning rod and bifocal eyeglasses.

Franklin served in Britain during 1757–1762 and 1764–1775. This was the period of British-American meetings about how the colonies should be governed. He represented and spoke

for the colonies in the British Parliament. When Franklin began his work in London, he thought Britain should continue to govern the colonies, and he once wrote in a letter, "There never was a good war or a bad peace." But by the end of his stay he was convinced that the colonies should break with Britain.

When Franklin returned to Philadelphia in 1775, he immediately became a delegate to the Second Continental Congress. He was a member of the committee to draft the colonies' Declaration of Independence, which led to the birth of the United States of America. Shortly after the Revolution began in 1776, Franklin was sent to France to win French support for the war. He was a popular figure and did much to win French aid. In 1787, he became a member of the Constitutional Convention, which created the American Constitution. Because he was then very old, he did not take an active part, but he urged the other representatives to create a legislature with two houses.

ALSO READ: AMERICAN HISTORY, AMERICAN REVOLUTION, CONTINENTAL CONGRESS, ELECTRICITY, GOVERNMENT, POSTAL SERVICE.

FRECKLES see SKIN.

FREDERICK, KINGS OF PRUSSIA Three kings of Prussia were named Frederick.

Frederick I (1657–1713) was the first king of Prussia. He followed his father to the title of "Great Elector of Brandenburg" in 1688. Then, in 1701, he crowned himself king of Prussia, with the permission of Holy Roman Emperor Leopold I. Frederick founded the University of Halle and Berlin's Academy of Sciences.

Frederick II (1712–1786) became known as Frederick the Great. Just after he became king in 1740, he began the War of Austrian Succession and also the Seven Years' War. He fought against the armies of Austria, France, and Russia. After the wars he kept part of Austria, called Silesia. He also gained more land for Prussia when he joined with Austria and Russia to conquer and divide up Poland. Frederick built a strong government and a powerful army. He also did much for his country's industry and farming. But he did not believe that the people could rule themselves. During his reign, the Academy of Sciences became an important center of learning again. The king invited philosophers and writers to visit his court.

Frederick III (1831–1888) became king of Prussia and emperor of a united Germany in 1888, but he died three months later. He took an important part in affairs of his country even while his father, Wilhelm I, was king. Frederick believed in government by elected representatives of the people. He married a daughter of the British Queen Victoria. Their eldest son later became Wilhelm II.

ALSO READ: AUSTRIA, GERMAN HISTORY, HOLY ROMAN EMPIRE, POLAND, VICTORIA.

___

FREEZING see REFRIGERATION.

___

FRENCH see ROMANCE LANGUAGES.

FRENCH AND INDIAN WAR

The French and Indian War, fought between 1754 and 1763, made North America British rather than French. It was not a war against Indians, but rather a fight between Britain and France for control of North America. Most of the Indians supported the French side in the war. The French and Indian War was part of the Seven Years' War.

The Seven Years' War was waged both in Europe and outside it. In Europe, France, Russia, Austria, and Spain fought against Britain, Prussia, and Hanover. The reason these countries fought was because both Austria and Prussia wanted to govern Germany. But Britain and France joined in because they wanted to become the world's most powerful nation. In North America, the British and French clashed head-on.

For many years before the war, the French firmly controlled Canada. They tried to gain control of the Ohio River Valley and the land west of the Appalachian Mountains. This threatened the British colonies of New York, Pennsylvania, and Virginia. People in those colonies felt they owned all the land to the west.

The French built Fort Duquesne (later to become Pittsburgh) where the Allegheny and Monongahela rivers join to form the Ohio River. Colonists in Virginia decided to stop the French. They sent 22-year-old George Washington, then a lieutenant

▲ *Frederick I (called "Barbarossa"), the first king of Prussia.*

▲ *Frederick II ("the Great") of Prussia. He made Prussia a major European power. A writer and composer, he encouraged artists of all kinds. He also gave the Prussian people more influence in the way their country was run.*

◄ *The Battle of Quebec (1759), was the turning point in the French and Indian War. General James Wolfe, commander of the British forces, died from wounds, as did his adversary, the commander of the French forces, the Marquis de Montcalm.*

FRENCH GUIANA

More than half the people in French Guiana live in the capital city, Cayenne. (Cayenne pepper is named for it.) Outside the capital there is only one person to every square mile of the country (0.4 per square km).

▼ *The subtropical coast of French Guiana where steamy rain forests meet the Atlantic.*

colonel, and his militia to attack the fort in 1754. But the French overpowered and defeated young Washington and his troops.

The French, using Indian allies and fighting methods, easily won early victories. Many frontier settlers in western New York, Pennsylvania, Maryland, and Virginia had to flee back to eastern settlements in the face of fire and tomahawk raids by the French and the Indians.

The British lost many battles, including those at Fort Oswego on Lake Ontario, Fort William Henry near Lake Champlain, and Fort Ticonderoga in New York. When William Pitt the Elder became Prime Minister of Great Britain in 1757, he pressed the war with new zeal. The British used their stronger navy to cut off French forces. The British could provide better supplies and replacements for their soldiers than the French. The British captured Fort Frontenac in 1758 and then overwhelmed Fort Duquesne. They forced the French to surrender at Fort Niagara and Fort Ticonderoga.

In the decisive battle of the war, the British General James Wolfe opposed the French Marquis de Montcalm on the Plains of Abraham near Quebec. Both generals were killed, but Britain defeated France. Britain gained all the land east of the Mississippi in what is now the United States, as well as part of Canada. As a result, the British heritage and the English language dominate the United States and most of Canada.

ALSO READ: BATTLES, FAMOUS; CANADA; QUEBEC; WASHINGTON, GEORGE.

FRENCH GUIANA France's overseas *department* (state) of French Guiana lies on the northeast coast of South America. It is bordered on the west by Surinam and on the south and east by Brazil. French Guiana is a little larger in size than the state of Maine. Maine's largest city, Portland, has almost as many people as in all of French Guiana. (See the map with the article on SOUTH AMERICA.)

The climate of French Guiana is rainy, hot, and humid. The land rises from lowlands along the coast to the thickly forested mountains of the interior. Most of the country is covered by rain forest, some of it completely unexplored. France used the region as a prison settlement for almost 100 years, until 1945. The most horrible—and most famous—prison was on Devil's Island off the northern coast.

The people of French Guiana speak French. But a few thousand native Indians and blacks living in the interior and recent immigrants speak other languages. Nearly all of the population are blacks, many descended from slaves brought into the country in the 1600's.

Most people live along the coast, where the capital city, Cayenne, is situated. Nearly half of all the people in French Guiana live in Cayenne. The town of Kourou, also on the coast, is the site of a spacecraft launching center operated by the French government. Some French Guianans are farmers. They raise bananas, rice, sugarcane, pineapples, cacao, manioc (cassava), and some livestock. Most of the people work in the mining and lumbering industries. Gold and bauxite (an ore containing aluminum) are mined and exported. Other important exports are wood-veneer products, timber, shrimp, and rum.

The coast of Guiana was first sighted by Christopher Columbus in 1498. The French established Cayenne as a permanent settlement in the early 1600's. Life there was made difficult by disease, Indian raids, and attacks by other countries. French Guiana was a French colony from 1817 until 1946, when it became an overseas department of France. Today, French Guiana is ruled by a French-appointed commissioner and an elected General Council of 16

FRENCH GUIANA

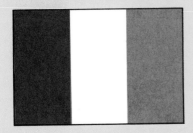

Capital City: Cayenne (38,000 people).
Area: 35,135 square miles (91,000 sq. km).
Population: 76,000.
Government: French Overseas Department.
Natural Resources: Bauxite, lumber.
Export Products: Shrimp, lumber.
Unit of Money: French franc.
Official Language: French.

members. It sends a representative to each of the two houses of the French Parliament.

ALSO READ: FRENCH HISTORY, SOUTH AMERICA.

FRENCH HISTORY Early people living in France were known as the *Gauls*. The Romans conquered them and made their lands into a Roman province in 51 B.C. During the 300's, tribes living to the east began invading the region. One group of invaders were the Franks, led by Clovis. They ended the Romans' rule in 481, and Clovis became king. Another great early ruler was Charles Martel. He fought Islamic invaders from Arabia. These invaders were defeated at Tours in 732.

Later in the 700's Charlemagne, Charles Martel's grandson, successfully extended the boundaries of his kingdom. He made a group of nobles his advisers. The king took away certain powers of the feudal lords and made them obey him. Charlemagne supported scholars and established many schools. The unification of the Frankish Empire temporarily ended with Charlemagne's death. But the lands were reunited in the late 900's.

▶ *Between 1804 and 1815, France was ruled by the Emperor Napoleon I, whose armies had conquered most of Europe.*

► *Joan of Arc receives the keys to the city of Troyes from the Dauphin (who later became King Charles VII) during the Hundred Years' War against the English.*

▼ *A French cavalryman of Napoleonic times. In those days the cavalry was the pride of most armies.*

Hugh Capet became Duke of France and the founder of the Capetian Dynasty of kings.

The Capetian kings forced the nobles to recognize their rule. They also improved the relationship between their country and the Church. The people gained the right to appeal to the royal courts in the late 1100's. A national army was established, and the royal treasury was strengthened. The nation's boundaries were extended. Such accomplishments transformed France into a leading European country. The dynasty ended in 1328 when King Charles IV had no male heirs.

King Philip VI, his cousin, became the new king and the first member of the Valois Dynasty. Nine years later, he found himself at war with England in what is known as the Hundred Years' War. Edward III of England believed that he should be the ruler of France. The war was waged, off and on, for 117 years. The English took away much territory from France. Joan of Arc, a young peasant woman who claimed to be guided by saints, finally led her country's army to a victory against the invaders. Following the Hundred Years' War, the king's advisers, known as the Estates-General, made reforms to help unify the country.

The 16th century was an unsettled one because two religious groups rivaled one another. The two groups were the Catholics and the Huguenots, a Protestant sect. Many Huguenots were massacred. The Catholic–Huguenot rivalry came to an end in 1598, when the Edict of Nantes was issued by Henry IV. His edict granted religious freedom and many civil rights to the French people.

Under Bourbon Rule Henry IV was the first ruler of the last French dynasty, the Bourbon. France became one of the most important European countries. During the reign of Henry IV's grandson, Louis XIV, the nation became a great military power and the cultural center of Europe. France was well administered, the navy became stronger, and industries developed. Land in North America, India, and the West Indies came under French control. Many writers, including Molière and La Fontaine, worked during this period. However, in 1685, the Edict of Nantes was revoked, causing many Huguenots to leave the country.

The French kings believed that one way to increase their nation's power was to go to war with other European countries. These wars were not always successful. Moreover, they were very expensive. The French people became increasingly unhappy at how the kings were ruling the nation. They demanded that Louis XVI call a meeting of the Estates-General to save the nation from bankruptcy. Mem-

RULERS OF FRANCE FROM 751 TO 1870

THE CAROLINGIANS

Pepin III (*le Bref*; the Short)	751-768
Charlemagne	768-814
Louis I (the Pious)	814-840
no king	840-843
Charles I (the Bald)	843-877
Louis II (the Stammerer)	877-879
Louis III	joint ruler 879-882
Carloman	joint ruler 879-882
	ruler 882-884
Charles II (the Fat)	885-887
Eudes (Odo) (not a Carolingian)	ruler 888-893
	joint ruler 893-898
Charles III (the Simple)	joint ruler 893-898
	ruler 898-922
	joint ruler 922-923
Robert I (not a Carolingian)	joint ruler 922-923
Rudolf of Burgundy (not a Carolingian)	923-936
Louis IV (Louis from Beyond the Sea)	936-954
Lothair	954-986
Louis V (the Sluggard)	986-987

THE CAPETIANS

Hugh Capet	987-996
Robert II (the Pious)	996-1031
Henry I	1031-1060
Philip I	1060-1108
Louis VI (the Fat)	1108-1137
Louis VII (the Young)	1137-1180
Philip II Augustus	1180-1223
Louis VIII	1223-1226
Louis IX (Saint Louis)	1226-1270
Philip III (the Bold)	1270-1285
Philip IV (the Fair)	1285-1314
Louis X (the Quarrelsome)	1314-1316
John I (the Posthumous)	did not reign
Philip V (the Tall)	1316-1322
Charles IV (the Fair)	1322-1328

THE HOUSE OF VALOIS

Philip VI	1328-1350
John II (the Good)	1350-1364
Charles V (the Wise)	1364-1380
Charles VI (the Mad)	1380-1422
Charles VII (the Victorious)	1422-1461
Louis XI	1461-1483
Charles VIII	1483-1498

Louis XII	1498-1515
Francis I	1515-1547
Henry II	1547-1559
Francis II	1559-1560
Charles IX	1560-1574
Henry III	1574-1589

THE HOUSE OF BOURBON

Henry IV	1589-1610
Louis XIII	1610-1643
Louis XIV (*le roi soleil*; the Sun King)	1643-1715
Louis XV	1715-1774
Louis XVI	1774-1792 (executed)
(Charles) Louis XVII	did not reign (died in prison 1795)

THE FIRST FRENCH REPUBLIC

National Convention (radical leaders of the Revolution)	1792-1795
Directory (a five-man board of moderate leaders)	1795-1799
Consulate (a three-man board led by Napoleon Bonaparte)	1799-1804

THE FIRST EMPIRE

Napoleon I (Napoleon Bonaparte)	1804-1814 *and* 1815
Napoleon II	did not reign

RETURN OF THE HOUSE OF BOURBON

Louis XVIII	1814-1824
Charles X	1824-1830

HOUSE OF BOURBON-ORLÉANS

Louis-Philippe	1830-1848

THE SECOND FRENCH REPUBLIC

Louis Napoléon (President)	1848-1852

THE SECOND EMPIRE

Napoleon III (Louis Napoléon)	1852-1870

From 1871 to 1940 France was governed under the Third Republic. The Vichy Government ruled during the years 1940-1944. Provisional Presidents between 1944 and 1946 were Charles de Gaulle, Félix Gouin, Georges Bidault, and Léon Blum. The Fourth Republic lasted from 1947 through 1959. The Fifth Republic, whose first President was Charles de Gaulle, started in 1959 and is still in existence.

bers of the Third Estate, or people belonging to the middle and peasant classes, wanted to limit the king's powers. They held a separate meeting and drafted a constitution for the country. Soon afterward, on July 14, 1789, they stormed the Bastille, a prison in Paris. This event marked the beginning of the French Revolution. The nobles and priests lost their privileges. The king, his wife Marie Antoinette, and many others were executed.

France During the 19th Century
After the Revolution ended in 1799, Napoleon Bonaparte, a brilliant and popular general of the Revolution, led France. He created the Code Napoleon, the basis of French law for more than 100 years. Hoping to make France part of an empire, he crowned himself Emperor Napoleon I in 1804. He eventually controlled much of Europe except Russia. But Napoleon was unable to stay in power because other European nations joined to-

The key to the Bastille—the Paris prison torn down by the French people during the French Revolution—was presented to George Washington by General Lafayette. It is on display at Mount Vernon, Washington's home in Virginia.

▲ *Louis Napoleon, who set up a second French Empire, with himself as Emperor Napoleon III, in 1852. He was the nephew of Napoleon I.*

▲ *Charles de Gaulle, leader of the Free French during World War II, and President of France 1959–1969.*

gether to defeat him. When he abdicated (resigned from) the throne in 1815, members of the Bourbon family ruled until 1848.

Louis Napoleon, nephew of Napoleon I, declared himself Napoleon III in 1852, and established the Second Empire. Meanwhile, many German states began uniting into a single country under the leadership of Prussia. The Prussians successfully went to war against the French to gain territory in 1870 and 1871.

Modern France After the French defeat, the Third Republic was established. France made alliances with European nations against Germany. It went to war against Germany and its allies in 1914. Much of the fighting was done on French soil, and nearly three-fourths of the French army suffered casualties. The Treaty of Versailles in 1919 brought peace to Europe for a few decades. But France's defeated neighbor, Germany, invaded again. This happened in 1940, a year after World War II began. Helped by its allies, France drove out the Germans in 1944.

The Fourth Republic was established a few years after the war ended. The country had to repair the damage that had been done. Certain French leaders began planning new ways of working with their European neighbors. Their plans led to the creation of the European Economic Community (Common Market). Meanwhile, former French colonies began to declare their independence.

Charles de Gaulle became his nation's president in 1958 when the Fifth Republic was established. A new Constitution gave de Gaulle many powers that earlier presidents did not have. He hired many new administrators to make the government function more smoothly. More housing was constructed, some changes were made in the educational system, and certain laws were updated. France became a nuclear military power. In 1969, de Gaulle resigned. Georges Pompidou became president until he died in 1974. Valéry Giscard d'Estaing was elected president. He was defeated in 1981 by François Mitterrand, a socialist. In 1986, however, a right-of-center government was elected to serve under Mitterrand.

For further information on:
Events, *see* CRIMEAN WAR, FRENCH REVOLUTION, HUNDRED YEARS' WAR, WORLD WAR I, WORLD WAR II.
Important People, *see* DE GAULLE, CHARLES; JOAN OF ARC; MARIE ANTOINETTE.
Places, *see* FRANCE, PARIS, VERSAILLES, WATERLOO.
Rulers, *see* CHARLEMAGNE; CHARLES, KINGS OF FRANCE; CHARLES MARTEL; HENRY, KINGS OF FRANCE; LOUIS, KINGS OF FRANCE; NAPOLEON BONAPARTE.

FRENCH REVOLUTION The French Revolution took place between 1789 and 1799. It brought many changes in the way that France was governed. The Bourbon family no longer ruled the country, and the average citizen gained many legal rights.

During the century before the Revolution began, the French government had faced many difficulties. The country had fought in various wars against its European rivals and had loaned money to the North American colonies during their revolution. Certain members of the royalty spent money unwisely. Various attempts to do something about the nation's debt were unsuccessful.

In May 1789, King Louis XVI called for a meeting of the Estates-General, which had not met for 174 years. This group represented the three major social classes. Priests belonged to the first estate, and the nobility belonged to the second estate. They had usually supported the

▲ *The storming of the Bastille. This event, which took place on July 14, 1789, heralded the French Revolution.*

king in the past. The remainder of the population—the majority—belonged to the third estate. They had often disagreed with the first and second estates, feeling that they were over-taxed and had no voice in govern-ment. The representatives wanted to talk about a change in the amounts people were taxed. They also wanted the common people to have greater rights. But the king made it clear that their meeting was about the country's finances alone.

The third estate was not happy with this and proclaimed a separate meeting, called the National Assem-bly. Some members of the other es-tates held opinions similar to those of the third estate, and came to the meeting. Food was scarce all over France at this time. People began rioting in Paris, and on July 14 they stormed and captured the Bastille, the royal prison. As a result of the rioting, members of the National Assembly drafted new laws. In August, they wrote and formally accepted the "Declaration of the Rights of Man and Citizen."

The Constitutional Assembly met to draft a new constitution, which was completed in 1791. The king lost many of his powers. Hereditary titles were outlawed, and trial by jury for criminal cases became required. The Catholic Church lost its lands and much of its power. Despite the new constitution, many people decided to take further action. They overthrew and imprisoned the king in August 1792. He was executed in 1793. This left France without any single leader. Members of the large group that gov-erned France could not agree with each other. The group failed to give equal rights to everyone, as the revo-lutionaries had originally wanted. Members of this group began to struggle for power. A group of radi-cals, the Jacobins, led by Maximilien Robespierre, seized control of the government. They imprisoned and killed many people who disagreed with them. The period became known as the *Reign of Terror*. It ended when Robespierre was arrested and executed.

A new constitution was put into effect in 1795. It stated that the Di-rectory, a group of five men, would govern France. But certain people living in Paris were not happy with the rights given them by the Con-stitutional Convention. When they rebelled, they were stopped by gov-

The 250 million dollars that it cost France to aid the Americans in the War of Independence helped to bankrupt Louis XVI and his reck-less court. This was the last straw for the people of France. The French Revolution began with the storming of the Bastille prison in 1789, only six years after the end of the American Revolution.

▼ *Three of the leaders of France's National Convention. From left, Georges Danton, Maximilien Robespierre, and Jean Marat. They set up the "Reign of Terror," during which thousands of their opponents were sent to the guillotine. Danton himself went to the guillotine in 1794, as did Robespierre. Marat was murdered in his bath by Charlotte Corday in 1793.*

▲ *Sigmund Freud, the Austrian doctor whose studies of the mind led him to create the theory of psychoanalysis.*

▼ *If you slide down a smooth slope you will go very fast, like this boy. There is very little friction to slow you down. But, if you try to slide down a rough slope, you won't get very far! This is because the friction between you and the slope is too great for you to be able to slide.*

ernment troops under Napoleon Bonaparte.

Meanwhile, France had been fighting a war against certain European nations and Great Britain since 1792. People were tired of disorder and uncertainty in government and their lives, and most had not gotten as much good from the Revolution as they had hoped. The Directory was overthrown, and Napoleon became one of the three members of the Consulate. In time, Napoleon became First Consul of France. He ruled the country like a dictator. He later became emperor. People preferred his strong leadership to a freedom that had led only to a lack of order and to fighting among politicians. But the Revolution had brought people much good. Serfdom was abolished, some large estates were broken up, and a new tax system was introduced. Many other social and economic reforms that were instituted are still a part of French law today.

ALSO READ: DICTATOR; FRANCE; FRENCH HISTORY; LOUIS, KINGS OF FRANCE; NAPOLEON BONAPARTE.

FREUD, SIGMUND (1856–1939)
Sigmund Freud was an Austrian doctor who explored the workings of the human mind. He developed *psychoanalysis*, which is both a way of treating *neuroses*, or mental disturbances, and a theory of how the mind works.

Freud was born in Moravia, now part of Czechoslovakia. When he was four, his family moved to Vienna, Austria. Freud entered the University of Vienna when he was 17. One day he attended a lecture on nature. He was so fascinated that he made up his mind to become a doctor.

Freud became interested in diseases of the mind. In 1885, he won a fellowship to study in Paris under the guidance of a doctor, Jean Martin Charcot, who was famous for his work on this kind of disease. The next

year, Freud returned to Vienna, married, and began to treat diseases of the mind.

Freud had great insights into the human mind. He taught that every person is born with certain needs, such as the need for food. These needs, he said, are *unconscious*—people are not aware of thinking about such needs. Freud named the part of the mind controlling these instinctive unconscious needs the *id*, and said that a person's id operates to give pleasure.

Freud also said that, as we grow up from infancy, we acquire an *ego*, a collection of memories and thoughts that help us deal with the world around us. We continue to grow, and from the teaching of our family and society, we develop a *superego*—a conscience. Our superego and id often push in opposite ways. Our ego usually reduces this conflict by helping us get pleasure without "hurting" our conscience.

But if a person's unconscious thoughts and needs are very strong, they may cause unusual behavior, or neurosis. Freud's treatment for neurosis is psychoanalysis ("examination of the mind"), a method for uncovering these unconscious thoughts and understanding how they cause problems. Freud taught that dreams—even dreams that seem to make no sense—are a very important clue to understanding the mind.

ALSO READ: DREAM, EMOTION, MEMORY, MENTAL HEALTH, NERVOUS SYSTEM, PSYCHOLOGY.

FRICTION Friction is the force that resists the motion of one object along the surface of another. Friction depends partly upon *how much* surface an object has. Suppose you have a square object and a round object weighing exactly the same and made of the same material. You try to push both objects along the surface of a

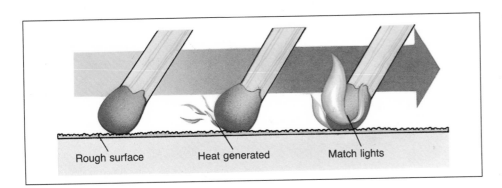

Rough surface | Heat generated | Match lights

◀ *Matches light because of
the heat produced by friction
as they are scraped along a
rough surface. This heat
makes substances in the
match's head catch fire.
Almost all matches today are*
safety matches. *The head of
the match only catches fire
when rubbed against a special
substance.*

floor. The square object will show a lot more friction (resistance to motion) than the round object, because more of the surface of the square touches the surface of the floor.

Friction also depends upon the type of surface an object has. Rough objects provide more friction than smooth objects. Sandpaper, rocks, and sticks have rough surfaces that produce a lot of friction. Teflon, soap, and ball bearings have slick, smooth surfaces and much less friction. Ordinarily, all objects have a certain amount of friction because nothing is perfectly smooth. However, at extremely cold temperatures, some substances show no friction.

Lubricating oil or grease reduces the friction of a surface. Automobile-engine parts rub against each other constantly, so oil is regularly added to the engine to reduce the amount of friction between moving parts.

Friction produces heat. When two rough objects are rubbed together rapidly, the friction between them causes them to get warm. Try rubbing your hands rapidly together and feel the heat that develops. People once used friction to start a fire by twirling a stick rapidly on a block of wood. The heat produced by friction ignited bark and leaves.

ALSO READ: CRYOGENICS, ENERGY, HEAT AND COLD, MOTION, PERPETUAL MOTION.

FROBISHER, MARTIN see ARCTIC, EXPLORATION.

FROGS AND TOADS Long before there were any people on the Earth, frogs and toads were hopping around. Frogs and toads are classified as *amphibians*, animals that spend the first part of their lives in water and their adult lives at least partly on land.

There are many different kinds of frogs and toads, from the tiny tree frog to the African giant frog, which can grow up to 26 inches (66 cm) long and weigh up to 10 pounds (4.5 kg). The largest North American frog, the bullfrog—6 to 8 inches (15 to 20 cm) long and about 1½ pounds (680 g)— is one of the champion jumpers. It can jump 20 times the length of its own body.

Frogs are found everywhere in the world but Antarctica, and toads everywhere but Antarctica and Australia. Some kinds of frogs and toads live in every state of the United States and in Canada, though the greatest number of kinds are found in the southeastern United States.

Some of these animals spend most of their lives in underground caves or abandoned mines. And certain *species* (kinds) of frogs never set foot on the ground. Their eggs are laid in rainwater in boat-shaped leaves of trees. The resulting tadpoles develop and swim about in these little pools, and the adult frogs spend their lives in the trees, eating tree-dwelling insects.

Mature frogs and toads breathe through lungs, as we do. But they are cold-blooded—that is, their bodies are only as warm, or as cold, as the air around them.

▼ *A tadpole becomes a frog
through a series of dramatic
changes. When it hatches from
its egg, it has no mouth. It
attaches itself to a leaf or a
stone and feeds on the remains
of its yolk. Soon it develops a
mouth, and a set of gills.
About three months later, it
develops lungs and loses its
gills. Soon it has legs, a
shorter tail, and a bigger
mouth. It is now a young frog.*

▲ *Male frogs make a loud sound at mating time to attract a mate. They do this by blowing up their vocal sacs with air.*

▲ *A toad sits motionless on the forest floor. If an insect flies within reach, the toad uses its long tongue to grab the insect.*

Arrow poison frogs of Central and South America produce a very powerful poison from glands in their skin. Indians use this poison to coat the tips of their arrows in order to hunt and kill animals more easily. The poison is so powerful that one millionth of a gram is enough to kill a person.

When it gets cold in winter, frogs and toads *hibernate* (spend the winter in an inactive condition, much like sleep) under the ground or in underwater mud. They need no food during this time, and, instead of breathing, they take in oxygen through pores (tiny openings) in their skin. In the spring, they "wake up" and make their way to fresh water to deposit their eggs. The female frog lays her eggs in clusters. The female toad lays hers in long strings. There may be anywhere from a few hundred eggs—laid by smaller kinds of frogs and toads—to thousands, laid by bigger species. Then the male spreads sperm on the eggs. The sperm fertilizes the eggs, making it possible for them to develop and hatch. Finally, the adult animals return to land.

You may confuse frogs with toads when you see them, because they do look similar. But there are several differences.

Frogs have smooth, moist, shiny skin, and they usually stay in moist areas. Their hind legs are developed for longer jumps than are toads' legs. They can escape from enemies this way, and often do so by jumping into water. Their tongues are lightning-quick, to catch fast-moving insects and other food, such as minnows.

Toads' skins are rough, dry, and somewhat lumpy. (The lumps, or "warts," once made people think that a toad could give warts to people who touched them, but this is not true.) Most toads can live in drier locations than can frogs. In fact, toads are found in desert areas except those few places, such as Death Valley, that are absolutely without water. The toad is less adapted for speed than the frog. Its hind legs are shorter, and its body is wider, heavier, and clumsier. But the toad has one superb advantage against its enemies. When a toad is attacked or frightened, glands in its skin ooze a bitter, slimy coating that stings the mouth of any bigger animal that tries to eat the toad. As for getting food, the toad's tongue is not so quick as the frog's. But the toad simply eats slower-moving food, such as crawling insects. Both frogs and toads, like many other animals, have *protective coloring*. They blend with their surroundings, and can easily conceal themselves from enemies.

ALSO READ: AMPHIBIAN, PROTECTIVE COLORING.

FRONTIER LIFE see PIONEER LIFE.

FROST On cold winter mornings, you often find the windowpanes of your house covered by feathery designs of ice. These icy crystals are frost or *hoarfrost*. Outside, you may find frost on almost anything.

Frost forms in much the same way as dew. When air cools, it must give up some of its water vapor (water in the form of a gas). When the air temperature is above water's freezing point, which is 32° F (0° C), the water vapor *condenses*, changing into dew (droplets of water). But when the air temperature is below freezing, the water vapor changes directly into ice crystals.

Sometimes the weather report predicts frost. This does not always mean that frost will form. (If the ground temperature is warm, it may not.) It means that frost could form because the temperature of the air will be below freezing. Temperatures that cause frost can kill plants by freezing them. Freezing the juices inside plant cells makes them expand and break the cell walls. If farmers know that frost is expected, they can cover their crops to keep the air around the crops warm.

■ **LEARN BY DOING**

Examine frost on a window with a magnifying glass. What does the frost look like? Go outside and try to find a frost-covered leaf. What shapes do you see? ■

ALSO READ: ATMOSPHERE, CRYSTAL, RAIN AND SNOW.

FROST, ROBERT (1874–1963) Robert Lee Frost was one of the most popular U.S. poets. Born in San Francisco, he was taken at the age of ten to New England. He later attended Dartmouth and Harvard colleges and worked as a farmer, newspaper editor, and schoolteacher. His first book of poems, *A Boy's Will*, appeared in 1913.

Frost spent much of his life on his farms in Vermont and New Hampshire. His poems show his love for the New England countryside and his feeling for its people. He used plain language to tell of common things and to make statements about nature, life, and death. Among his most famous poems are "Birches," "Mending Wall," "Stopping by Woods on a Snowy Evening," and "Home Burial." His poetry is sometimes light-hearted and amusing, and sometimes bitter, full of pain and loneliness.

Frost received the Pulitzer Prize

▲ *In this wintry glade, evergreen branches are laced with frost crystals.*

Robert Frost is supposed to have said: "A diplomat is a man who always remembers a woman's birthday, but never remembers her age."

◄ *The 1814 Frost Fair on the Thames River, London, England. The frost was so severe that the frozen river supported marquees and even campfires.*

▲ *Robert Frost, popular and internationally acclaimed American poet.*

for poetry four times. In 1961, he read his poem "The Gift Outright" at the inauguration of President John F. Kennedy. He published many books of poetry. His last collection of poems, *In the Clearing*, was published in 1962, when Frost was 88 years old.

ALSO READ: LITERATURE, POETRY.

FROZEN FOOD see FOOD PROCESSING.

FRUIT One of the most delicious and healthful types of food is fruit. Fruits may be eaten raw, cooked, dried, canned, or preserved. Citrus fruits (such as oranges, grapefruits, and lemons), tomatoes, and strawberries are excellent sources of vitamin C. Most fruits contain large amounts of vitamins A and B. The growing, processing, packaging, and shipping of fruits is one of the biggest industries in the United States.

What Is Fruit? Plants reproduce through the spreading of seeds. These small seeds are produced and protected within a female organ of the flower, called the *ovary*. Inside the ovary, the seeds develop. The ovary grows larger and larger. A mature ovary is a fruit.

The cavities in the fruit where the seeds are developed are called *locules*. The *endocarp* surrounds the locules. In some fruits, such as peaches and

▲ *Blackberries grow wild almost everywhere in the United States. They are delicious when they are fresh. But they are also good as preserves and in pies.*

cherries, the endocarp becomes a hard and stony pit. Inside the pit are one to three seeds.

The middle layer is called the *mesocarp*. This is usually soft and pulpy, and forms the flesh of the fruit. The outer layer is the *exocarp*. These three layers compose the entire wall of a fruit, the *pericarp*.

Have you ever noticed the "seams" on some fruit? When a fruit is not harvested for commercial use, it will drop off the tree or bush. It will then "split at the seams." The seeds are now ready to grow where they are, or be carried by the wind or animals to reproduce wherever they may fall.

Growing Fruit In colonial days, families raised fruit trees mostly for their own use. Women canned fruit and made jams and jellies for their families. It was not necessary to own much land to supply fruit for one family. For example, a standard apple tree grows to a height of about 25 feet (7.5 m) and needs about 40 square feet (3.5 sq. m) of land in which to grow.

Thanks to the work of agricultural scientists, it is now possible to grow many small fruit trees on a small plot of land. These little fruit trees are called *dwarfs*. Sixteen dwarf fruit trees can be planted on the same space needed for one standard apple tree! Of course, apples are not the only

▼ *The hot damp weather in Central America and the West Indies is just right for growing bananas. The plastic bags provide protection from insect pests.*

fruits that come from dwarf fruit trees. Among other varieties of dwarf fruit trees are pear, peach, cherry, apricot, and plum.

The fruit from dwarf trees is just as good as that produced from standard fruit trees. In many cases, the fruit from dwarf trees is better in color and larger in size. Another advantage of dwarf fruit trees is that they don't take long to reach their full growth. A good crop of fruit can be harvested as early as three years after planting a young dwarf tree. A standard apple tree takes seven to 20 years before it produces a good crop! With good care, a dwarf apple or pear tree will produce high-quality fruit for 40 years.

Growing a fruit tree is a complicated job that requires much attention. The soil must be properly prepared and fertilized when the tree is planted. The earth between fruit trees must be *cultivated*—the ground must be broken so there will be good drainage and so the soil will hold moisture. Fruit trees must be *pruned*, or trimmed, annually, usually in the spring. Old or unhealthy branches must be cut off so that new branches will have room to grow. Regular spraying, or dusting, with special chemicals helps the tree to resist insects and disease, although some people prefer not to spray in order to have *organic* fruit.

Oranges and other citrus fruits can be ruined by frosts. Growers must put oil heaters or other kinds of burners among the trees, to be used if the weather turns unseasonably cold.

In colonial times, no refrigeration systems for fruit storage existed. Fruit spoiled when it was shipped long distances in slow-moving wagons or sailing ships. During the 19th century, scientists developed new methods of fruit growing and storage. The invention of railroads and steamships made it possible to ship fruit to distant places quickly enough to make fruit growing profitable. Thousands

DIFFERENT KINDS OF FLESHY FRUITS

Cherries

Drupes
The fruit has a fleshy outer layer and a hard inner layer (the stone). The actual seed is inside the stone. Blackberries and raspberries consist of several small drupes (drupels) lightly joined together.

Plum   Peach

Blackberry

Raspberry

Tomato

Orange

Berries
The entire fruit is fleshy and contains many seeds. It is usually formed from several carpels, each segment of the fruit being formed from one carpel.

Grapes   Gooseberry

Pomes
The true fruit is the core. The edible part is the swollen receptacle.

Apple   Pear

of trees were planted, and fruit farming grew into a big business.

Harvesting, or gathering, fruit at the right time is very important. If fruit is picked when it is too ripe, it will spoil quickly. If it is picked when it is too green, it will not ripen properly and will not be of good enough quality to be sold in the markets. Usually the fruit is picked in what growers call the "hard ripe stage." That means the fruit is firm and almost ripe. By the time it reaches the stores, it will be ripe and attractive to customers.

Another important factor that must

Bananas and seedless oranges are examples of types of fruit that develop naturally without producing seeds. Flowers of other plants, such as tomatoes and pears, can be sprayed with plant hormones so that they too produce seedless fruit.

▲ *Drying fruit in Morocco. Dried fruit can be stored for long periods without becoming rotten.*

Pectin, a substance like gelatin that is used to thicken jellies and jams, comes from fruit. It is obtained from the inner rind of oranges and other citrus fruits. Pectin is also a by-product when apple cider is made.

be considered when growing fruit trees is the local soil and climate. The soil must be good, and the climate must be suitable for the particular type of fruit tree. Trees must be planted at different times of year in different parts of the country. In the northern half of the United States, experts recommend planting in the spring. Fruit trees can be planted in the spring or fall in the Pacific Coast states and in the southern part of the country.

Apple trees grow best in the central United States, the Northeast, and the Pacific Northwest. Pear trees produce well in Michigan and New York, and in the Pacific Coast states. Peaches grow well in Arkansas, California, Colorado, Illinois, Michigan, and, of course, the "Peach State," Georgia.

The Fruit We Eat Americans eat apples, oranges, and bananas more than any other kind of fruit. Bananas are imported, mostly from Central and South America. But apples, oranges, and other fruits are grown widely in the United States. Most of the oranges and other citrus fruits we eat come from California, Florida, and states bordering the Gulf of Mex-

ico. Pineapples are an important fruit crop of Hawaii.

Much of the fruit we eat has been canned, frozen, or made into jams and jellies. Some fruits are squeezed for their juice. Others, such as apples, apricots, plums (prunes), and grapes (raisins), may be dried.

Modern methods of growing, processing, refrigeration, and transportation have made it possible for us to enjoy fruits of many different kinds in many different forms. They are available to us, no matter where we live, the whole year round.

ALSO READ: FOOD, FOOD PROCESSING, NUTRITION, SEEDS AND FRUIT.

FRUIT FLY see DROSOPHILA.

FUEL A few logs burn in the hearth of a hut in the hill country of northern India. A racing car speeds around the track at Indianapolis, and gasoline burns constantly in its engine. A natural-gas flame shines brightly inside the heater of a home in Connecticut. Logs, gasoline, and natural gas are different kinds of fuel, materials burned to produce heat or power. Fuel may be solid, liquid, or gas.

Early Fuels *Wood* was probably the first fuel that people used. Ever since early times, wood has been burned to produce heat for warmth and for cooking.

Coal was used as fuel more than 3,000 years ago. For about a century and a half after the invention of the steam engine, coal was the most important fuel for producing heat to make steam. Coal was fuel for steam railway locomotives, steamships, and for the many kinds of steam-driven machines in factories. Coal is still used to produce about half the electricity generated in the United States today.

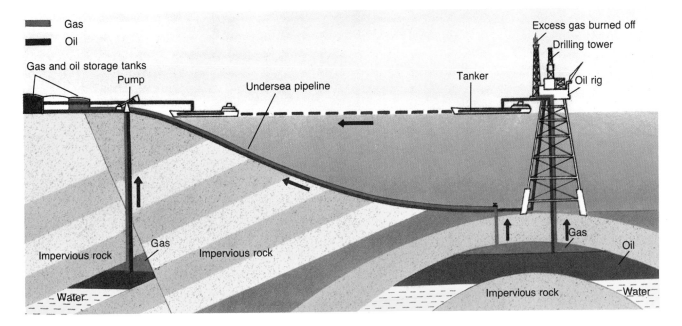

Gas
Oil

Gas and oil storage tanks
Pump
Undersea pipeline
Tanker
Excess gas burned off
Drilling tower
Oil rig
Impervious rock
Gas
Impervious rock
Gas
Oil
Water
Impervious rock
Water

Peat and *lignite* are two coal-like fuels. Peat is a dark-brown material formed by plants (usually mosses) that have decayed in water. It is partly carbon (the main element of coal). Dried peat is used both for heating houses and for providing industrial power in Ireland and in parts of the Soviet Union. Lignite, or brown coal, was also formed from decayed plants. It has more carbon than peat, but much less than black coal. It is used to produce steam for generating electricity in those parts of the United States near where it is mined.

Coke and *charcoal* are created in the absence of air. Coke is a solid made by heating coal. It is used mainly in steel making, and sometimes in domestic hearths. Charcoal is made from wood. Charcoal is almost pure carbon. As a fuel, its main use in the United States is for outdoor cooking in grills and at campsites. In many Latin American countries it is the chief fuel used in cooking. All of these fuels are solid. But other fuels are liquids and gases.

Most liquid fuels come from *petroleum*, the oil that comes from oil wells. Gasoline, kerosene, diesel oil, and the oil used in oil-burning house heaters are all separated from petroleum. Diesel locomotives have entirely replaced coal-burning steam lo-

comotives in the United States. Most ships now have oil-burning engines, rather than steam engines.

Huge space rockets may burn a fuel mixture of liquid oxygen and hydrogen. Both of these liquids must be kept at very low temperatures because they are gases at ordinary temperatures and no rocket could be built large enough to hold the gases.

Natural gas is a fuel that is widely used in the United States for heating buildings, making steam, and also for cooking. Natural gas is found deep underground at the top of petroleum pools. Also, gas comes from coal when it is made into coke, and from petroleum when it is distilled. Another fuel gas, *producer gas*, is made by passing a mixture of air and steam over a bed of glowing coal or coke.

The material (for example, uranium) that is put into nuclear reactors is called *atomic fuel* or *nuclear fuel*. It produces great amounts of energy but does not chemically burn. Nuclear reactors are used to generate electricity and to power some submarines.

Nonnuclear fuels are compared by measuring the amount of heat a certain quantity of fuel produces. The amount of heat is measured in *British thermal units* (BTUs) or in joules (J).

▲ *Natural gas and oil are important fuels. They are found (usually together) in cavities deep among the rocks of the Earth's crust. Often the cavities are below the ocean bed, so that huge oil rigs are needed to raise the gas and oil.*

▼ *Liquid oxygen is a fuel used to power space rockets. To make it, air is liquefied by putting it under pressure and making it expand, several times over. But air is a mixture of gases, notably nitrogen. The nitrogen and other gases are allowed to boil off, leaving pure liquid oxygen.*

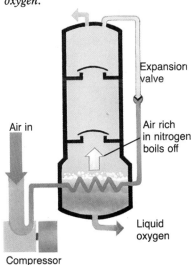

Expansion valve
Air in
Air rich in nitrogen boils off
Liquid oxygen
Compressor

▲ *Radioactive substances are used as fuel to make electricity. Atomic reactors such as this one are producing an increasing amount of electricity in many nations, although they have their dangers. In 1986, there was a major accident at the reactor at Chernobyl, in the Soviet Union, and harmful radiation was spread over a wide area.*

▼ *Robert Fulton, U.S. inventor and engineer.*

About 1,055 J equals 1 BTU. One BTU is the amount of heat needed to raise the temperature of one pound of water one Fahrenheit degree. Cost is also important. Even though a small amount of one fuel may produce enough heat, it may cost far more than a larger amount of another fuel.

ALSO READ: COAL, DISTILLATION, ENERGY, ENGINE, FIRE, HEAT AND COLD, NUCLEAR ENERGY, PETROLEUM.

FUEL CELL   A fuel cell is a special kind of electric battery. An ordinary battery like those in a tape player or flashlight contains some chemicals. The chemicals react together to produce electricity. When all the chemicals in the battery have reacted, the battery is dead.

A fuel cell also makes electricity from chemicals, which are called its fuel. The chemicals are fed into the fuel cell to make it work, so that it need never run out of chemicals. It continues to produce electricity for as long as it gets fuel.

The fuel cell was invented in 1959 by the British scientist Francis T. Bacon. Its main use is in manned spacecraft. Fuel cells supplied electricity in the Apollo spacecraft that flew to the moon. They also produce electricity in the space shuttle. These fuel cells use hydrogen and oxygen as fuel. Inside the fuel cell, the gases react together to produce electricity. The waste product is pure water, which the astronauts can drink.

FULTON, ROBERT (1765–1815) In the 1700's and early 1800's, sailboats and barges carried cargoes up and down New York's Hudson River. But Robert Fulton changed the scene in 1807. He put a new kind of boat on the Hudson. Chugging and belching black smoke, the boat moved against the current and against the wind. It was the *Clermont*, the first commercially successful steamboat.

Robert Fulton was born on a farm in Lancaster County, Pennsylvania. He became a talented painter. But he was also an inventor and an engineer. He invented a machine for dredging the bottom of rivers and a machine for making rope. He also built a submarine, the *Nautilus*.

Sometime before 1803, Fulton began to work on a way of making a steam engine propel a boat. His idea was to make the engine turn large paddlewheels on each side of the boat. He built the *Clermont* at a shipyard near the East River in New York City. Fulton's completed boat steamed up the Hudson River to Albany on August 17, 1807. People laughed at the *Clermont* and called it "Fulton's Folly." But the trip was successful, and many other engineers soon began to build similar boats. Fulton's *Clermont* marked the beginning of the end of sailing ships as the best way of water transportation.

ALSO READ: SHIPS AND SHIPPING.

FUNGUS   On a walk in the woods, you may come upon bright orange shelves growing on the side of a fallen log. They are one kind of fungus. A doctor may prescribe penicillin for an infection. The penicillin comes from a *mold*, another kind of fungus. Yeast, which makes bread light and fluffy, is still another kind of fungus. Other familiar family members are mushrooms, puffballs, and plant-rusts. As you can see, some fungi are important to us—as foods or as medicines. Others are very poisonous. Fungi are very rich in protein, and scientists today are working to see if they can breed certain types of fungi to be the "miracle foods" of tomorrow.

All fungi are plants. Fungi do not have roots, stems, leaves, or flowers. Fungi also lack chlorophyll, the green coloring matter that enables most other plants to produce their own food. Fungi must take their food from other plants or animals, living or dead. Some kinds of fungi, *saprophytes*, feed on dead plants or animals. The rest of the fungi live on or in living plants or animals, using some part of them as food. These fungi are *parasites*. They may cause great harm to their host.

Fungi reproduce in several ways. In asexual reproduction, a fungus produces spores in small containers called *sporangia*. When the spores are ripe, the sporangia burst open and the spores fly out. A spore is something like the seed of higher plants. Wind, water, and insects can carry the spores long distances. When a spore rests on material that a fungus can use for food, the spore grows into a new fungus plant.

In sexual reproduction, a male and a female cell unite to form a large spore. These spores, called *perfect spores*, can survive conditions of extreme dryness or cold. When conditions improve, they can grow into new fungus plants.

Yeasts are very small fungi. Yeasts reproduce by budding. A yeast cell grows a bud (a little bump), which then splits off as a separate cell.

Many fungi, including rusts, mil-

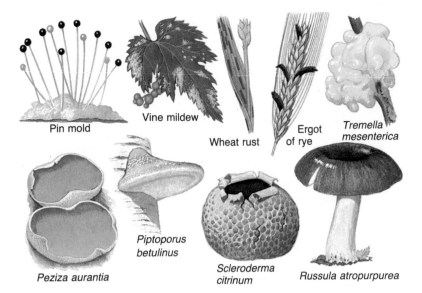

Pin mold

Vine mildew

Wheat rust

Ergot of rye

Tremella mesenterica

Peziza aurantia

Piptoporus betulinus

Scleroderma citrinum

Russula atropurpurea

dews, and smuts, can cause diseases. Rust fungi have nothing to do with the rust that eats away iron and steel. That is a chemical process. These fungi are plant parasites that take nourishment from plants they live on or within. They drain so much energy that their plant hosts die.

■ LEARN BY DOING

The black, orange, and bluish—or greenish-gray—patches that often appear on stale, damp bread are mold. Mold is one fungus that is easy to study.

Moisten a piece of bread and leave it on a table overnight. The next day put the bread into a glass jar and cover the jar. After a few days, you will see fuzzy patches growing on the bread. Examine a patch with a magnifying glass or the low-power lens of a microscope. You will see a tangle of threadlike growths that cover the bread and grow down into it. Note that small rods topped by dark knobs grow upward from the threads. The threads serve much the same purpose as roots. Through them, the mold gets nourishment from the bread. The dark knobs contain spores. Mold spores in the air fell on the bread you left on the table. ■

A slime mold is a very interesting kind of living thing. During one part

▲ *A fungus is a threadlike organism that reproduces by means of spores. Some produce their spores in large fruiting bodies that we call mushrooms, toadstools, brackets, cups, puffballs, and jellies. Shown here are various forms of fungi.*

▼ *The body* (mycelium) *of a fungus is made of a mass of fine threads called* hyphae. *The hyphae produce enzymes that break down food. Sometimes the hyphae weave together to form mushrooms and toadstools.*

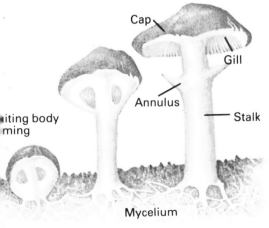

Cap

Gill

Annulus

Stalk

iting body
ming

Mycelium

▼ *A mold is a type of fungus. A mold of* Penicillium *is used to make the drug penicillin, a powerful germ-killer.*

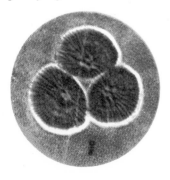

▲ *Fungus spores are everywhere in the air. This is why moist food becomes covered in molds so quickly.*

of its life, it acts like a fungus, growing sporangia and reproducing by spores. During the other part, a slime mold oozes slowly from place to place and eats solid food particles, in the manner of an amoeba, which is an animal.

Mushrooms are large fungi, usually umbrella-shaped. Some are good to eat. Others, often called *toadstools*, are very poisonous. Only experts can tell which mushrooms are good and which can kill you. Never eat mushrooms that you find growing wild.

ALSO READ: ANTIBIOTIC; CELL; FLEMING, SIR ALEXANDER; MUSHROOM; PARASITIC PLANT; PLANT; YEAST.

FUR Not all mammals are soft and furry like a kitten. An adult elephant has only a few hard bristles of hair on its back. Most mammals, however, have a full covering of fur.

The fur on a mammal's body grows from special groups of cells, called *follicles*, in the skin. Each hair is a rod of a type of protein called *keratin*—the same substance that makes claws, fingernails, hoofs, and horns. Each follicle contains a tiny muscle that can raise the hair growing from it.

The main function of fur is to keep the body of the warm-blooded mammal at an even temperature. Fur traps air that is warmed by the body. The trapped air serves as an insulating blanket to keep the animal warm. In warm weather the muscles in the follicles raise the hairs and the trapped

▲ *Baby seals are covered in soft fur. The annual slaughter of baby seals for their fur has aroused much controversy.*

air is released. The hairs may also rise if a mammal is about to fight, so that the mammal appears large and more fierce to its enemy.

There are actually two kinds of fur. Most hairs make up the short *underfur*. This is soft and thick and does most of the work of insulating. Other, longer hairs are called *guard hairs*. They generally carry the color markings, such as stripes or spots, and they protect the softer underfur.

The hair follicles in skin also contain glands that give off oil, which makes fur waterproof. This is especially important for sea mammals (such as seals) that have no thick layer of fat to keep them warm. Whales and dolphins have thick fat layers and do not need fur coats. Some whales do not have a single hair on their bodies.

The fur of some mammals, such as the ermine and the Arctic fox, changes color with the seasons. Scientists are not really sure what makes

▼ *The European mink is much valued for its soft fur. There are many farms that breed minks for their fur.*

these animals turn white in winter and dark in summer. It may be a combination of cold and fewer hours of daylight as the seasons change. Similar changes cause mammals to acquire thick coats in autumn and shed them in spring.

Furs to Wear   Since people discovered that fur could keep them warm, some animals have been hunted for their coats, or pelts. Some animals, such as the sea otter, have been hunted almost to extinction. In recent years, more and more people have opposed the killing of animals for their fur.

Beautiful "fake" furs made of synthetic materials are now being manufactured. Ecologists hope that the synthetic furs will take the place of real furs and help save the needless annual slaughter of many beautiful and some increasingly rare fur-bearing animals.

The Fur Traders   Many English, Dutch, and French people came to North America to search for furs in the 1600's. They were called "fur traders." Some trading companies, like the Hudson's Bay Company, were established to do business in furs. Many colonists and, later, U.S.

▼ *Fur coats being spray cleaned in a Japanese factory.*

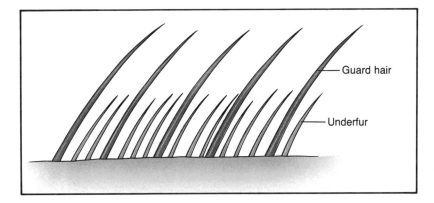

▲ *Typical arrangement of a mammal's fur.*

citizens became fur traders, too. The skins and furs were shipped to Europe, where they were traded for goods and supplies needed by the people living in the New World.

The fur traders went inland from the seacoast by following Indian trails and valleys, and by paddling canoes up many North American rivers. Many traded for furs with Indians who brought them to trading posts and forts. Trading posts were often built where two bodies of water came together. Some trading posts, such as Detroit and St. Louis, later became cities.

The fur traders gave the Indians inexpensive jewelry, guns, and liquor for the furs. Early colonial laws forbade trading guns and ammunition to the Indians, but the fur traders did so anyway. The English fur traders stayed mostly at their trading posts, but the French often traveled into the wilderness to trap animals or to find Indians who had furs for trade. They used canoes that could float along shallow streams to bring back the furs they obtained far from the nearest trading post or fort. While searching for furs, they explored much of the Great Lakes region and central Canadian provinces.

Deerskin, or *buckskin*, was one of the most common animal pelts sought by the fur trader. Buckskins were widely used to make leather trousers. The skins and furs were traded for food and other supplies in many colonial seaports. The slang expression "buck," which means a dollar, comes

During the Middle Ages in England there were strict rules regarding the wearing of furs. Sable, ermine, marten, and genet could only be worn by the royal family and the court. Less valuable furs were worn by the middle classes, and the least valuable furs such as rabbit and cat were worn by the common folk. Furs were worn mostly by men.

▲ *A chair used in religious ceremonies during the reign of Tutankhamen, an ancient Egyptian pharaoh (king). It is made of wood and covered with gold.*

from "buckskin." Beaver hats were so popular in Europe that "beaver" became a slang expression for hat. Fur traders also sought the skins and furs of muskrats, minks, bears, foxes, buffaloes, otters, and seals.

Fur trading continued long after the American colonies became the United States. The Lewis and Clark Expedition helped the fur traders because it showed them new routes they could take. The Pacific Northwest became a hunting ground for North American and Russian fur traders.

Many people made their fortunes as fur traders. The U.S. businessman, John Jacob Astor, established the American Fur Company in 1808. In 1810, Astor founded a fur-trading fort named "Astoria" along the Columbia River. The American Fur Company was highly successful in competing with traders from other countries. Astor became a millionaire.

ALSO READ: CARSON, KIT; COLUMBIA RIVER; EXPLORATION; HAIR; LEWIS AND CLARK EXPEDITION; MAMMAL; SKIN.

FURNITURE People have not always needed furniture. Each day primitive people moved from place to place, hunting for food. Their "homes" were wherever they happened to stop and rest for the night.

When people began to raise crops, they also began to live in one place. Soon they became aware of the need for furniture to make their lives more comfortable. The earliest furniture probably consisted of stools and headrests carved from single pieces of wood.

Ancient Furniture The ancient Egyptians made fine furniture with simple, graceful lines (shapes), rich ornamentation, and carved inscriptions. Since wood was scarce and expensive, furniture was more common in the homes of nobility and priests.

Greek furniture-makers also created graceful furniture, but not so straight and simple as Egyptian furniture. The Greeks used different kinds of wood, such as oak, cypress, and cedar. They decorated pieces of furniture with precious metals. They of-

Chinese Ming hardwood chair from about 1500

16th-century Italian folding armchair

Chair in the house of a 16th-century merchant

Chippendale settee from 1772

Sheraton sofa from the mid-18th century

Upholstered U.S. rocking chair of the 1850's

Mahogany high chair dated 1860

Mackintosh chair made in 1901

ten used cushions, which they covered with fine fabrics.

The Romans borrowed their furniture designs from the Greeks, adapted the designs to their own taste, and developed what is called the Greco-Roman style of furniture. The Romans used much bronze and marble, especially in the construction of tables and chair legs. Greco-Roman furniture had many fancy ornaments, and Greco-Roman cushions were even more luxurious than those of the Greeks.

The Middle Ages Furniture was scarce throughout the Middle Ages. A home was usually one large room. In the room stood plain tables and benches, straw-filled mattresses, and large storage chests, called *coffers*. During the Crusades of the 1100's and 1200's, people traveled to the

Middle East. There they saw furniture that was both useful and beautiful. They returned home with many new ideas for more comfortable living. They made cabinets with doors and sometimes with drawers. Shaped backs were added to stools. Wooden beds were made to raise the new feather mattresses off the floors. Woven fabric (tapestries) covered walls, adding warmth, color, and beauty to rooms.

In the late 1200's, the 1300's and the 1400's, the *Gothic* style of furniture was dominant in northern Europe. Gothic furniture was chiefly made of oak, a heavy wood. Skilled workers decorated the furniture by carving figures and designs into the wood. Despite the carvings, Gothic furniture was solid and simply framed. It was sometimes painted.

▲ *This elegant room in Joseph Manigault's house in Charleston, South Carolina, provides a fine display of beautifully-made chairs, tables and cabinets.*

Furniture was so scarce in Europe during the Middle Ages that it was quite common for a visitor to bring along his or her own bed and other personal articles.

▲ *The Great Bed of Ware, in England. Made of oak, it was built in the late 1500's and is more than ten feet (3 m) square. The mattress rested on ropes, not springs. Beds in those days were treasured possessions, and were often left as legacies to friends or relations.*

▼ *A wooden chair decorated with a colorful tapestry. It was made during the 1700's.*

Furniture Changes In the 1500's, furniture-makers began to study the styles of ancient Rome, and created heavy, elaborate pieces of furniture decorated with classical ornament. The wood they used was often walnut. Also, inexpensive furniture was made for poorer people to buy.

Large chests, formerly used by nobles and clergymen while traveling, were set on legs and became permanent pieces of furniture. The legs made it difficult to reach the lid, so an Italian designer set drawers into the lower part of the chest, and the first chest of drawers was made. Other designers added arms, backs, and cushions to low chests, creating the first sofas. Furniture became more ornate. It was often painted in bright colors. Some furniture was covered with fine gold paint.

During the 1500's and 1600's, explorers brought Chinese and Japanese furniture back to Europe. Around 1700, Oriental influence in furniture styles began to be seen in decorated panels and screens, often covered with *lacquer*, a glossy coating.

In the 1700's French furniture-makers created light and graceful pieces, using fancy kinds of wood with brass, tortoiseshell, and porcelain decoration. Gilded mirrors were

hung in fashionable homes. Much of this furniture was destroyed during the French Revolution. While Napoleon ruled France, classical Greek and Roman furnishings were again stylish. Chairs had backs shaped like lyres, or small harps. Couches had rolled wooden ends.

English Furniture Mahogany was the favorite wood in Britain in the 1700's. By that time, many gentlemen (and some ladies) owned books, so bookcases were designed. During Queen Anne's reign, chairs had less decoration and were made for more comfort. Wealthy ladies began to collect Chinese porcelain figures to exhibit in new china cupboards. Ladies also copied the French custom of receiving visitors while resting in bed. They ordered beautiful "four-poster" beds—beds with a tall post at each corner—covered with canopies and curtains of damask and tapestry. Chairs were made wider in order to accommodate the ladies' hoopskirts.

Furniture styles were usually named for rulers. But the designs of Thomas Chippendale were so unusual and so beautiful that his own name was used. He drew ideas not only from all the styles around him, but also from China and Japan. Much Chippendale furniture stands on ball-and-claw feet. It is often coated with lacquer in Oriental fashion.

Until the 1800's, much furniture was *commissioned*. If people wanted a specific piece of furniture, they had a designer or carpenter make it for them. Poor people built their own furniture. In the 1800's, machinery began to be used to make furniture. Since no individual maker was responsible for each piece, furniture often looked ugly and clumsy.

North American Furniture Early settlers brought furniture from their European homes. As the colonists needed more furniture, craftsmanship flourished. Usefulness, not style, was important. Furniture-makers used woods they could find easily, such as cedar, beech, chestnut, hickory, pecan, and pine. *Joiners*, or carpenters, made plain pine tables and chairs with straight backs and woven seats. Beds were simple wooden frames with ropes strung from side to side.

As U.S. furniture-makers became more skilled, they learned to take European styles and change them to make truly American designs. However, furniture in the styles of the English makers, especially Chippendale, Thomas Sheraton, Robert and James Adam, and George Hepplewhite were common in the wealthy colonial household. Some furniture was imported, too, from England and even from France. George Washington and Thomas Jefferson both owned French furniture.

Probably the best known early U.S. maker was Duncan Phyfe. He studied the works of English and French cabinetmakers and changed their designs. In 1800, he made much of the furniture for the President's house in Washington. Most of the furniture that Phyfe built was destroyed when the British burned Washington in 1814.

Modern Furniture Almost every piece of furniture used today can be grouped under five headings: (1) furniture for rest, (2) furniture for work, (3) furniture for storage, (4) furniture for controlling our surroundings, (5) furniture for decoration. The fifth group is much more recent than the others, although many decorative articles of furniture also have other uses. For example, carpets and draperies not only decorate a room, but often help keep it warm (or cool) or help reduce noise.

When furniture is made today, designers still think first of usefulness and then of ornamentation. Most modern furniture designers feel that a room should be simple and comfortable. New manmade materials have added

variety and practicality to furniture.

One quite recent innovation is the use of plywood. Plywood is made by joining thin layers (plies) of wood, with the wood grain in each layer at right angles to that in the adjoining layers. It is good for large, flat surfaces because it is strong and does not shrink or swell. Also much used today is particle board. In this material wood particles are bound together with resin. Another modern material is plastic. Plastic coatings resist spots and stains. Plastic can be made to look like fine wood, or it can be molded into nearly any shape a designer can think of.

Wood furniture is made in *machine shops*. The seasoned wood is cut into the proper lengths and planed to the desired thickness. Then holes are drilled so that the pieces can be fastened together. *Hand shops* do the finishing work, such as attaching cabinet doors and fitting drawers. Many kinds of finishes, such as shellac, varnish, oil, stain, paint, and lacquer, are used on furniture.

Most of the furniture made in the United States is made in North Carolina. Other centers of the furniture industry are in Massachusetts, Pennsylvania, Michigan, Illinois, and New York.

ALSO READ: ANTIQUE, WOOD.

▲ *The furniture in modern homes is designed both to be comfortable and to look good. The tubular steel chair to the front of the picture is considered a classic in design.*

The Shakers, a religious sect named for their trembling during worship, were also skilled furniture designers. They came to New York in 1774 from England and spread out as far west as Indiana. Their sparse, functional furniture pieces are now collectors' items.

In Gabon, November is the wettest month, when the country has an average of 15 inches (380 mm) of rain. This is more than three times the U.S. average in August, our wettest month.

GABON The republic of Gabon lies on the Atlantic in west-central Africa. It has beautiful lagoons, grassy plains, and dense tropical forests. Gabon's interior is made up of high plateaus and mountains. (See the map with the article on AFRICA.)

Gabon has a hot and humid climate. Rainfall is heavy. Most of the Gabonese people live near the coast or along the rivers. Libreville, the capital and chief port, is on the north coast. There are many tribal groups in the country. A few pygmies, less than 5 feet (1.5 m) tall, live in the jungles of the south. The people mainly work in the forestry and mining industries. Mahogany, ebony, and other trees are cut down for export. Gabon is rich in mineral resources. The principal minerals being extracted are oil, manganese, iron ore, and uranium. Natural resources, foreign investment in the country, and government programs have made Gabon one of the more prosperous African countries. Its population, however, is only about one million.

Portuguese sailors landed in Gabon

GABON

Capital City: Libreville (257,000 people).
Area: 103,347 square miles (267,667 sq. km).
Population: 1,000,000.
Government: One-party republic.
Natural Resources: Oil, manganese, iron ore, uranium.
Export Products: Oil, metals, lumber.
Unit of Money: Franc of the African Financial Community.
Official Language: French.

about 1470. A slave trade was later set up in the region. English, Dutch, and French ships came for slaves until slave trading was stopped in 1814. The French took over the country in the late 1800's. Gabon then became part of French Equatorial Africa. The country became independent on August 17, 1960. Now the people elect a national assembly and a president who serves a seven-year term.

The famous mission hospital founded by Albert Schweitzer in 1913 is located at Lambaréné on the Ogooué River in western Gabon. It was run by Schweitzer until he died at age 90 in 1965.

ALSO READ: AFRICA; PYGMY; SCHWEITZER, ALBERT.

GAGARIN, YURI (1934–1968)

This Russian pilot was the first man in space. He was a cosmonaut (astronaut) for the Soviet Union. Yuri Gagarin rocketed into space from a launch site in Siberia on April 12, 1961. His spacecraft, *Vostok I*, orbited (circled) the Earth once. Gagarin went higher and faster than any man before him. He traveled as high as 200 miles (320 km) above the surface of the Earth. His fastest speed was more than 17,500 miles per hour (28,160 km/hr). His historic trip lasted 108 minutes. Curiously, the flight of *Vostok I* aided the U.S. space program, because the United States was spurred to catch up with the Soviet Union.

Yuri Gagarin was born near Smolensk in the Soviet Union. He graduated from a Soviet air-force training school in 1955. Gagarin asked for training to become a cosmonaut. He was chosen and began learning about spaceflight. After the flight of *Vostok I*, Gagarin continued to train as a cosmonaut, but he was killed in a jet-plane crash on March 27, 1968.

ALSO READ: SPACE TRAVEL.

GAINSBOROUGH, THOMAS (1727–1788)

Look at the portrait of Master John Heathcote in the long dress little boys wore in the 1700's. He is standing self-consciously, holding a large hat and carrying a small bouquet. This is how he posed in 1774 for Thomas Gainsborough, one of Britain's greatest painters.

At that time, Gainsborough was living in Bath, England, where he was very busy painting portraits. He had been born in Sudbury, in Suffolk. At age 13, he went to London to study until he was 21. He soon became a very successful portrait painter. Actually, his great love was landscape painting, but his portraits were in such great demand that he had to spend most of his time on them.

John Heathcote's mother asked Thomas Gainsborough to paint the boy's picture, and Gainsborough refused. But Mrs. Heathcote brought the boy to Gainsborough's studio anyway. When the painter saw the handsome lad, he could not send him away. John would much rather have been out playing ball or flying a kite than posing for an artist. But his brothers and sisters had all died in an epidemic, and his mother wanted very much to have his portrait painted—in case something happened to him, too. Gainsborough

▲ *Yuri Gagarin, the Soviet test pilot who became the first person to go into space.*

After Yuri Gagarin had circled the Earth on his historic flight, he landed in a field within 7 miles (10 km) of the planned spot.

◀ Master John Heathcote, *a painting by Thomas Gainsborough, is now at the National Gallery of Art, in Washington, D.C.*

On the Galápagos Islands live 14 kinds of finches. These birds all have similar bodies, but show an amazing variety of beak shape and use. These variations helped Charles Darwin support his theory of evolution.

painted the boy's picture larger than lifesize. He posed him with his left foot forward and holding a hat, similar to the way he had posed *Blue Boy*, another famous portrait, a few years earlier. See the highlights on the blue taffeta sash that give richness to the picture. Note the softness of the boy's pink and white complexion. Gainsborough was quick to see the inner qualities of his subjects. He caught John's shy, frank manner and his faint smile.

Gainsborough's style of painting was widely admired and imitated by painters in many countries. He became a founding member of the British Royal Academy at the age of 41, but in 1784, he left the organization after an argument.

ALSO READ: ART HISTORY.

GALÁPAGOS ISLANDS Most people know that penguins live in icy regions near the South Pole. But did you know that penguins are also found near the equator? The little Galápagos penguin lives very far from Antarctica. Its home—a group of Pacific islands called the Galápagos—lies on the equator, about 600 miles (965 km) west of Ecuador, South America. Penguins live there because the cool

Humboldt Current is rich in fish, their main food.

Some animals of the Galápagos Islands—such as the giant tortoise—are not found anywhere else in the world. Other unusual creatures include a four-eyed fish, a rare sea bird called the flightless cormorant, and the marine iguana, a lizard that dives into the ocean for seaweed. Charles Darwin, a British scientist, studied the unusual wildlife of the Galápagos in 1835. His research showed him facts that led to his theory of evolution.

The Galápagos Islands include five large islands, eight smaller ones, and over 40 islets and shoals, all formed from volcanic rock. A Spanish navigator discovered them in 1535. Pirates used the islands as hideouts during the late 1600's, and North American ships stopped there in the 1700's. Sometimes animals were left there. Wild dogs, cats, donkeys, goats, and pigs now roam some islands. They provide meat and skins for the islands' inhabitants.

Ecuador formally claimed the Galápagos Islands as a territory in 1832. The people who live there today make their living by fishing or by growing coffee, potatoes, and lemons. Ecuador made the islands a national park and wildlife refuge in 1959 to protect the rare animals and plants.

ALSO READ: DARWIN, CHARLES; ECUADOR; EVOLUTION; TURTLE.

GALAXY see ASTRONOMY.

GALILEE, SEA OF The Sea of Galilee was the scene of some of the most famous incidents in the life of Jesus Christ. The New Testament of the Bible tells that once, on the banks of the sea, Jesus fed a crowd of 5,000 people with just five loaves of bread and two fishes. He is also said to have walked on the sea and calmed the waves in a storm. On another occa-

▼ *The Galápagos Islands formed about 2 million years ago. Since that time, several unique species have evolved there. As well as the famous finches noted by Charles Darwin, there are giant tortoises, marine iguanas, land iguanas, and flightless cormorants. At one time each island had its own race of giant tortoises, but during the 1600's and 1700's visiting sailors killed them for food, and some races have disappeared completely.*

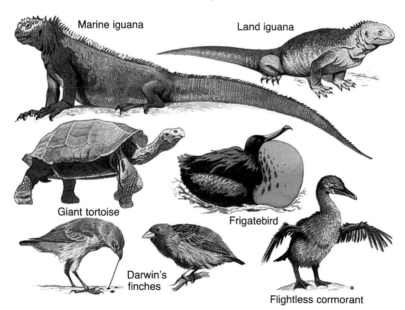

Marine iguana

Land iguana

Giant tortoise

Frigatebird

Darwin's finches

Flightless cormorant

▲ *A fisherman with his net, early in the morning on the Sea of Galilee. He is following a tradition that dates back to before the time of Jesus Christ.*

sion, Jesus met several fishermen casting their nets in the Sea of Galilee. He convinced them that they should give up fishing and become his chosen followers, or disciples. Fishermen much like Simon (later called Peter), Andrew, James, and John still make a living fishing in the Sea of Galilee. Today, these fishermen use gas lamps to attract schools of fish at night, and they pull in silvery catches of a fish called *mousht*. This six-inch (15 cm) long fish is also often called "St. Peter's fish."

The Sea of Galilee, also called Yam Kinneret, Lake of Gennesaret, or Lake Tiberias, is a freshwater lake with some salt content. It lies about 700 feet (210 m) below sea level and is fed and drained by the Jordan River. Water from the sea is used by Israel to irrigate the surrounding region and the Negev Desert to the south. Wheat, cotton, vegetables, and fruit are grown in the region around the Sea of Galilee.

ALSO READ: ISRAEL.

GALILEO GALILEI (1564–1642)

In 16th-century Europe, most people believed exactly what was told or taught to them—by books, schools, or the Roman Catholic Church. Galileo Galilei helped to free people's minds from these constricting limits.

Galileo studied astronomy, mathematics, and physics in his hometown of Pisa, Italy, and later became a teacher of mathematics. He suggested that a pendulum could be used to measure time after he had studied a swinging lamp in the Pisa Cathedral. He also studied the laws of falling bodies and the laws of motion. Galileo said that the laws of the universe could only be known by measurement—length, weight, shape, and time. You might say that Galileo gave science the idea of "time" as a new and powerful tool. He questioned accepted "scientific" knowledge of that age, saying most of human understanding of the world was based on unproven ideas.

In 1609, Galileo built the first telescope for astronomical use. He observed and recorded for the first time sunspots, the craters of the moon, the moons of Jupiter, and the numerous stars of the Milky Way. His discoveries led him to believe that the Earth moved.

In 1632, Galileo published a book in which he supported Copernicus's theory that the Earth and other planets moved around the sun. Religious leaders were angered by this idea. At that time the Church taught that the Earth was the center of the universe. The book was condemned by the Church and its sale was forbidden. Galileo was put on trial and forced to disclaim his ideas in public. At the end of his trial, Galileo is said to have muttered, "E pur si muove" (Even so it [the Earth] *does* move). The Church sentenced him to live in seclusion for the rest of his life.

Galileo did *not* invent the telescope, microscope, thermometer, or the

▲ *Map of the Middle East showing the Sea of Galilee.*

A popular legend tells of Galileo dropping different weights from the top of the Leaning Tower of Pisa in Italy to test the speed with which they fell. This story is probably not true. We know, however, that he rolled balls of different weights down a slope and timed how long they took to reach the bottom.

▲ *Galileo, the great Italian physicist and astronomer.*

▲ *Luigi Galvani, the Italian scientist who discovered that electricity is involved in the movement of muscles.*

When Vasco da Gama reached the port of Calicut in India, he prepared gifts for the ruler. The ruler laughed and declared them unfit for a king. So da Gama sold his goods for a cargo of spices. When he reached Lisbon he sold his cargo for sixty times the cost of the whole expedition.

▼ *Vasco da Gama, the Portuguese explorer who was the first to sail from Europe round the Cape of Good Hope to India.*

pendulum clock, but he did lay the foundation for modern experimental science. Galileo greatly enlarged human knowledge of the world and the universe.

ALSO READ: COPERNICUS, NICOLAUS; SCIENCE.

GALLEON see SHIPS AND SHIPPING.

GALLUP, GEORGE see OPINION POLL.

GALVANI, LUIGI (1737–1798) Luigi Galvani was an explorer in the study of electrical currents. His work led to Volta's discovery of the battery and laid the foundation for the study of "animal electricity." The *galvanometer*, a device for measuring small electric currents, is named for him.

Galvani was born in Bologna, Italy, and he studied law and medicine there. Then he became professor of anatomy at the University of Bologna. One day, his wife, Lucie, noticed a peculiar thing about the legs of a dead frog that were lying on top of a metal table. The legs twitched and jumped when she touched them with a knife. She called her husband. Galvani watched in amazement as the dead legs twitched. He had to find out why.

Galvani conducted many experiments. He hung frog legs from copper hooks attached to the railing of his balcony. The wind blew the legs, which twitched each time they touched the iron railing. Galvani decided that the frog legs moved because an electric current was produced. But he thought the current was caused by the frog. He said that all living animals contain electricity, which disappears soon after the animal dies. This part of Galvani's idea was wrong. Electricity did cause the

legs to twitch, but the current was not produced by the frog's legs. Instead, it occurred when the two different metals—like the table and the knife—were connected through the frog's body.

ALSO READ: BATTERY, MUSCLE, NERVOUS SYSTEM.

GAMA, VASCO DA (about 1469–1524) Vasco da Gama, a Portuguese explorer, was the first to find a route by sea from Europe to India. Da Gama was encouraged by Portugal's king, Manuel I, to find a new sea route to get to the riches of Asia.

Another Portuguese, Bartholomeu Dias, had sailed in 1488 south down along the west coast of Africa until he reached the Cape of Good Hope and sailed around it. Da Gama took 170 men on four ships and followed Dias's route in 1497. He came ashore on the East African coast and found an Arab pilot, Ibn Majid, who guided him across the Indian Ocean to India.

The rulers of India gave da Gama a cold reception. They were suspicious of the Europeans. Arab traders were also anxious to avoid competition for India's riches. But the Portuguese

▼ *Vasco da Gama's ship rounding the Cape of Good Hope.*

persisted. Da Gama made two more trips to India. He also became the viceroy, or ruler, of the Portuguese colonies in India, the first European settlements in that country.

Columbus's discovery of the Americas turned Spanish attention west, across the Atlantic. Da Gama's discovery of a sea route to India turned Portugal's attention to the east. His explorations soon led to trade and colonization, and great wealth for Portugal. Da Gama ranks with Columbus as an important explorer.

ALSO READ: DIAS, BARTHOLOMEU; EXPLORATION; INDIA.

GAMBIA The smallest nation on the continent of Africa is the Republic of Gambia, which is smaller than Connecticut. Gambia is a narrow strip of land on the western coast of Africa. It is surrounded by the Republic of Senegal, except for its coastline on the Atlantic Ocean. Gambia includes the island of Saint Mary at the mouth of the Gambia River. The country extends about 200 miles (320 km) inland along either side of the Gambia River, but it is only about 20 miles (32 km) wide. (See the map with the article on AFRICA.)

Gambia has a hot, humid climate. The temperature often reaches 110° F (43° C). The capital city is the busy port of Banjul, on Saint Mary's Island. Oceangoing ships can travel from here up the deep Gambia River for about 150 miles (240 km).

Most Gambians are poor and earn their living from farming. They grow rice, maize (corn), sorghum, and peanuts (Gambia's most important crop and chief export). In recent years, tourism has increased. New hotels have been built, creating more jobs for Gambians.

Europeans first came to the area in the 1400's. Gambia later became a colony of Great Britain. The country won self-government in 1963 and complete independence on February 18, 1965. The people elect a president and the 35 members of their House of Representatives. Gambia is a member of the Commonwealth of Nations. In 1982, Gambia agreed with its neighbor Senegal to work closer together. They united to form the Confederation of Senegambia, but they kept their own separate governments.

ALSO READ: AFRICA.

GAME BIRDS Game birds live nearly everywhere in North America, from fields to forests to deserts to city parks, and even to the bitter cold grasslands of the Arctic. These birds are all chickenlike, land-living birds. All have short, heavy bills and short wings. They usually prefer walking or running to flying, and their long sturdy legs carry them quickly about on their search for insects and seeds.

▲ Baskets ready for loading on ship are stacked by Oyster Creek in Gambia.

The ruffed grouse is a noisy bird during the nesting season. The male "drums" with his wings at such a speed that you can see nothing but a feathered blur. The sound produced is something like the rumble of distant thunder.

GAMBIA

Capital City: Banjul (44,500 people).
Area: 4,361 square miles (11,295 sq. km).
Population: 800,000.
Government: Republic.
Natural Resources: No major minerals.
Export Products: Peanuts, palm kernels, fish, hides and skins.
Unit of Money: Dalasi.
Official Language: English.

▲ *The partridge is a popular game bird. It originated in Europe but has since been introduced in many other countries.*

Grouse Ten species of grouse live in North America. Most of these medium-sized birds live in northern woodlands. But the *sage grouse* lives on open plains, where it feeds mainly on sagebrush. The name of the *prairie chicken* tells you where this grouse lives. The *willow ptarmigan* lives on the barren, cold Arctic islands of northern Canada. Its diet consists mainly of willow leaves.

Quail Quail are small birds. Full-grown males are usually only eight inches (20 cm) long. The *scaled quail* is a common resident in dry semi-deserts in the American southwest. The *California quail* spends summers on mountainsides all along the west coast, from Mexico to Washington state. These birds move to the warmer foothills each winter. They do not fly. Instead, they make this journey—a distance of up to 50 miles (80 km)—on foot.

Farmers east of the Rocky Mountains have an excellent helper, the *bobwhite*, North America's most common quail. These birds devour huge quantities of harmful beetles, potato bugs, and grasshoppers, and a single bobwhite gobbles thousands of weed seeds each year.

Turkey This bird is almost 3 feet (91 cm) in length. Wild turkeys look much like barnyard turkeys but are more streamlined. Turkeys roost in trees at night, but they are poor fliers who run from danger. They eat fruit, seeds, and acorns. They once lived in woodlands all over the United States.

▲ *A willow ptarmigan revealed against the sparse spring vegetation of its Yukon homeland.*

Chachalaca This Central American native lives in thickets and woods in southern Texas and in Mexico. It usually perches on branches. Early in the morning and again at dusk, you can hear the chachalaca's call—it loudly repeats its name.

Other Game Birds Three game birds—the chukar, the gray partridge, and the ring-necked pheasant—were brought to the New World from Europe.

The *chukar* is a partridge. It lives in open, rocky land west of the Rocky Mountains. Its flight is very strong. The male's call is "chu-kar."

The *gray partridge* lives near farmlands. It is about the same size as the chukar—10 inches (25 cm) long. It is also a good flier.

The *ring-necked pheasant* lives in woods, hedges, and cornfields in many parts of North America. Of all the game birds, only the turkey is larger. Pheasants fly well—but only for short distances. They roost in trees and eat seeds and berries.

ALSO READ: BIRD, GARDEN BIRDS, PIGEON.

▼ *The pheasant is a game bird now found in many parts of the world. The males are bigger and much more brightly colored than the females.*

GAMES What's your favorite game? Both children and adults like to play games. Many of the games they enjoy are centuries old, and different variations of them are played in many parts of the world. For example, hide and seek is played in almost every country in the world—under different names, of course. Many sports, such as baseball, can be played as games—just for fun. Some games can only be played in certain places—indoors or outdoors, perhaps, or on special fields or courts. It would be rather dangerous to play baseball in the living room! Equipment, such as balls, rackets, cards, or dice, is needed to play some games. Although some games require luck, others demand skill. Sports, even simple ones like croquet, require skill. Card games usually depend on luck. But difficult card games, such as bridge, depend on a combination of skill and luck.

ALSO READ: CARD GAMES, CHILDREN'S GAMES, DICE, SPORTS, WORD GAMES.

▼ *Some games just develop, while others are invented. This Islamic picture shows the invention of the board game backgammon.*

GANDHI, INDIRA PRIYADAR-SHINI (1917–1984) Indira Gandhi was prime minister of India from 1966 to 1977, and again from 1980 to 1984. She was born in Allahabad, India. Her father was Jawaharlal Nehru, the first prime minister of independent India. In 1942 she married Feroze Gandhi, who died in 1960. As a member of India's Congress Party, she first held government posts in the 1960's. In 1966 she was chosen to be prime minister. In 1977, she lost power and, for a time, her seat in Parliament. But she returned, as leader of a reformed Congress (I)—for Indira—Party, for another term as India's premier.

Indira Gandhi worked to strengthen India's role as a leader of the nonaligned and underdeveloped countries. She led India to military victory against Pakistan in 1971. At home, breakaway movements, including Sikh extremists, opposed her. In October 1984, she was assassinated by Sikh gunmen. Her son, Rajiv, succeeded her as India's prime minister.

ALSO READ: INDIA; NEHRU, JAWAHARLAL.

GANDHI, MAHATMA (1869–1948) To the people of India, Mohandas Gandhi is thought to be the father of their nation. They named this small, thin man Mahatma, which means "Great Soul." He believed in peace and brotherhood, and felt that the way to achieve these goals was to be nonviolent, and unafraid. Above all things, he practiced love and tolerance for all humans. Many people in India were influenced by his views. He was never elected to an office, but he is known as one of the world's great figures.

Using his methods, Gandhi helped win India its freedom from the British. He also brought changes to the lives of many Indians who lived in

▲ *Indira Gandhi was India's prime minister from 1966 until 1977, and from 1980 until her assassination in 1984.*

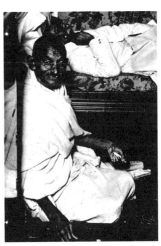

▲ *Mahatma Gandhi, the great Indian leader. He led a nonviolent campaign to free India from British rule.*

terrible conditions. Gandhi lived like a simple peasant. He ate very little food, and sometimes went on fasts, when he ate no food at all.

Gandhi was the son of an official in the small town of Probandar in India. His family practiced the Hindu religion, and, according to the custom, he was married at the age of 13 to an 11-year-old girl. Gandhi studied law in London and later went to South Africa, where he stayed for 21 years to work for Indian rights. He led workers in peaceful strikes against racial discrimination. Gandhi was jailed many times, for a total of seven years.

While Gandhi was attending a prayer meeting on January 30, 1948, he was assassinated by a man who disagreed with him politically. His death was mourned by the entire world. A great Indian poet, Tagore, said, "He will always be remembered as one who made his life a lesson for all ages to come."

ALSO READ: HINDUISM, INDIA.

GANGES RIVER The Ganges is the longest river in India, flowing a distance of 1,557 miles (2,507 km). It begins its course in the Himalaya Mountains of northern India, collect-

ing water from the melting snow and glaciers. The river flows in a southeastern direction, gathering additional water from its tributaries. It flows through a narrow gorge until it reaches the city of Hardwar, where it enters a large plain. The river becomes wider until it flows into the Bay of Bengal. (See the map with the article on INDIA.)

The river plain is large and fertile. Wheat is grown in the northern part of the region, and rice is grown in the southern portion. This area is one of the most densely populated in India. Large cities, including Calcutta and New Delhi, are here. Oceangoing ships cannot travel far inland, but smaller boats can, making the river a water highway.

Most Indians who belong to the Hindu faith believe the Ganges is sacred. They believe its waters can cure various ailments and purify their souls. Millions make pilgrimages to Vārānasi (Benares), Hardwar, and Allahabad, three holy cities on the riverbanks. Flights of steps, called *ghats*, lead down to the water at various locations. These steps are used as a place to worship, to cremate the dead, and to scatter their ashes upon the water.

ALSO READ: HINDUISM, INDIA.

GARBAGE see WASTE DISPOSAL.

GARDEN BIRDS Some birds have learned to live near human beings. They make their nests in trees and bushes near houses, or nest in birdhouses that people build for them. These birds seek food in backyards, lawns, and gardens. You usually see them in parks and schoolyards. These birds are sometimes called garden birds.

Garden birds include robins, bluebirds, bluejays, song sparrows, English sparrows, purple grackles, pur-

▼ *A crowded scene on the banks of the Ganges River. Hindus believe that the river is sacred.*

▲ *A female great spotted woodpecker feeding her young. Adult woodpeckers feed on grubs that they find in the bark of trees.*

Lark bunting

American robin

Mockingbird

Wood thrush

Cactus wren

ple martins, redheaded woodpeckers, house wrens, mockingbirds, and hummingbirds. If you live near woods and open fields, many other birds may come near your house. Among them may be starlings, barn-swallows, mourning doves, Baltimore orioles, tree sparrows, flickers, red-winged blackbirds, catbirds, and many kinds of finches.

If you live in the northern half of the United States, you may see a number of interesting birds, especially in the winter. Among them are chickadees, cardinals, bluejays, juncos, snow buntings, white-breasted nuthatches, tufted titmice, evening grosbeaks, and cedar waxwings.

The best way to attract birds to your house is to feed them. Winter is the best time to feed birds, because in that season birds' natural food is scarce or more difficult to find. But

you can attract birds during the rest of the year, too. When birds learn that they can always get food at a certain place, they will return there. Birds usually feed in the morning and evening. But if they find food, they will eat at any time of the day.

Birds eat cracked corn, peanuts, and the seeds of millet, sunflower, hemp, squash, pumpkin, cantaloupe, and honeydew melon. They also enjoy eating crumbled doughnuts, dried bread, crackers, and dog biscuits. Nuthatches and chickadees like peanut butter. Cedar waxwings eat dried currants and raisins. Woodpeckers, nuthatches, and chickadees like *suet*, a hard, fatty tissue that comes from cattle and sheep. You can buy suet in the supermarket. Wire the suet down, so that a bird cannot carry a whole piece away. Make sure no cats can reach the place you put the suet!

▲ *Black-capped chickadees range over most of North America. They are easily attracted to pine trees and swampy thickets.*

1037

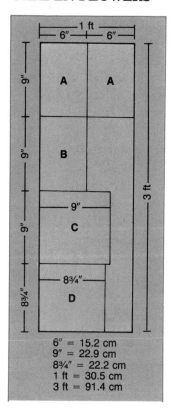

6" = 15.2 cm
9" = 22.9 cm
8¾" = 22.2 cm
1 ft = 30.5 cm
3 ft = 91.4 cm

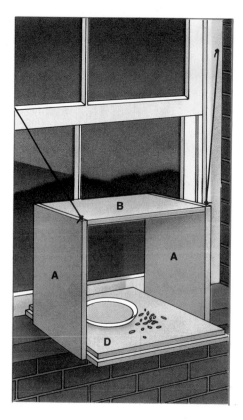

SOME GARDEN FLOWERS

Annuals
Alyssum
Marigold
Nasturtium
Snapdragon
Sunflower
Verbena
Zinnia

Biennials
Canterbury bell
English daisy
Forget-me-not
Foxglove
Hollyhock
Pansy
Sweet William

Perennials
Chrysanthemum
Columbine
Delphinium
Iris
Oriental poppy
Peony
Primrose

Bulbs
Crocus
Daffodil
Lily
Tulip

■ LEARN BY DOING

You can make a bird feeder and attach it to a windowsill. First get a piece of plywood one-half inch (1.25 cm) thick and at least three feet (90 cm) long and one foot (30 cm) wide.

Saw two pieces of plywood shaped like those marked *A, A* in the picture above left. The length and width of the pieces are given in the diagram. These pieces will be the sides of the feeder.

The piece marked *B* will be the top of the feeder. Piece *C* will be the bottom. It is wider than the top. One inch (2.5 cm) of the extra width goes at the back of the feeder to provide a space to drive nails. These nails are used to attach the feeder to the windowsill. Two inches (5 cm) stick out in front, making a "front porch."

Piece *D* will be like the piece *C* you cut for the bottom, but it should be one-fourth inch (0.6 cm) smaller in length and width than *C*. It is a removable bottom that you can take out and clean every few days.

When you have cut the pieces of wood to size, nail them together so that the feeder looks like the one in the diagram. Use thin nails. Drive two large nails into the removable bottom near its rear edge. These will make it easier to take the removable bottom out for cleaning. Drive two other large nails halfway into the top near the front corners. These are for attaching wires to help support the feeder.

With your parents' permission, nail the feeder to the windowsill, and attach the wires or string to the nails on top. Then hammer two nails halfway into the sides of the window frame, above the roof of the feeder. Finally, attach the other ends of the wires to these nails.

When the feeder is in place, put food and a saucer of water into it. When the birds arrive, do not stand too close to the window, or you will frighten them away. ■

ALSO READ: BIRD, GAME BIRDS, NATURE STUDY.

GARDEN FLOWERS All flowers were once wild flowers. Many were considered so beautiful that people planted them near their homes. These became garden flowers. Over the centuries, gardeners have made many of these flowers more attractive by changing their size, color, and shape. By combining the best features of closely related plants, they breed new plants called *hybrids*. In this way, hundreds of new varieties of garden flowers have been bred.

Almost all garden flowers are *herbaceous*. This means that they do not have woody stems covered by bark. However, some garden flowers, such as spirea, are woody.

Flowers called *annuals* grow from seeds, bloom, produce new seeds, and die, all in one growing season. To grow these flowers again, more seeds must be planted the next season. In most parts of the United States, seeds are planted in the spring and the flowers bloom in the summer. In the warmest states, annuals can be planted at any time of the year. Most annuals are easy to grow, so they are favorites with gardeners.

Flowering plants called *biennials* live for two growing seasons, bearing flowers during the second season. Gardeners usually plant biennials in midsummer to bloom during the next spring or summer.

Perennial flowers live for many years, blooming each growing season. Some perennials produce seeds; some have roots that put out new shoots that grow into new plants; and some do both. Most perennials are planted in spring, as soon as there is no more danger of frost. Some may be planted in the fall. They bloom more abundantly each year.

Bulbs are large underground buds swollen with food. The stored food gives plants that grow from bulbs a good start the next growing season. Most bulbs look like onions or garlics. *Tubers* and *corms* are swollen, fleshy underground stems that also store food. Tubers look like long, crooked potatoes. Gardeners usually call tubers and corms "bulbs," too. Bulbs can be dug up, shipped long dis-

tances, stored, or replanted. Bulbs are perennials. Daffodils and tulips are two well-known plants that grow from bulbs.

In the article on GARDENING, you will learn how to raise plants. Try growing a flowerpot or two of your favorite garden flowers. If you plant annual seeds, you will have beautiful flowers in just a few weeks.

ALSO READ: BULB, FLOWER, FLOWER FAMILIES, GARDENING, PLANT BREEDING.

▲ *This colorful border of annuals and shrubs includes fuchsias, nasturtiums, petunias and marigolds.*

▼ *A selection of garden flowers that can be found growing in the United States.*

Sweet pea

Hibiscus

Camelia

Forget-me-not

Peony

Native sunflower

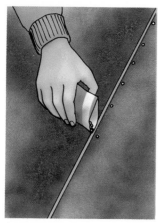

▲ *Some vegetables like beets can be planted in furrows. Plant a seed every two inches (5 cm) about three-fourths of an inch (2 cm) deep.*

GARDENING A famous Englishman, Francis Bacon, wrote, "God Almighty planted the first garden. And indeed it is the purest of human pleasures." Gardening is one of the most popular hobbies in North America. Millions of people spend much time and effort growing flowers, trees, fruits, vegetables, and grass. Gardening is a pleasure you can share in, whether your garden grows in a single flowerpot or on several acres of ground.

Plants to Grow Flowers are the plants that give a garden most of its color and fragrance. Some flowers live only one summer. Gardeners must plant them from seeds every spring. Other flowering plants live for two summers. Gardeners must plant them in the middle of one summer so that they will have flowers during the next summer. Still other plants live for many years, flowering every summer.

Some plants have flowers all summer, but most bloom only for a short time. Some, like certain rosebushes, have flowers only once during the early summer, but others bloom several times. Good gardeners learn how long after planting they can expect a flower to bloom. They can work out a timetable of flowers, so there will always be some in bloom. Sometimes

▲ *Tender plants such as young cabbages should be stored in a cold frame to protect them from the cold. In warmer weather they can be transplanted outdoors.*

gardeners plant seeds in pots indoors at a special time and replant them outdoors before the plants bloom.

Trees provide beauty and shade, and some supply fruits and nuts. Very few home gardeners grow trees from seeds, because this method requires more care and time than they usually want to give. Instead, most home gardeners buy trees from a *nursery*, where trees, shrubs, and plants are raised and sold.

A tree grows slowly when compared to a flower, but a tree may live for hundreds of years. A tall, sturdy tree is a magnificent reward for gardeners who have spent many years taking care of it. They must fertilize and prune it properly, as well as fight off diseases and insects that attack it.

Many gardeners do not grow vegetables, although raising them is as much fun and no more trouble than growing flowers. Peas, peppers, cabbages, turnips, spinach, corn, onions, carrots, potatoes, tomatoes, watermelons, and cantaloupes are some of the fruits and vegetables you can grow in a home garden. Tomatoes, onions, and peppers can be raised in a window box. Tomatoes may even grow in a flowerpot. Sometimes, when the weather is still cool, gardeners plant

▼ *A plant nursery where people can buy plants that are already partly or fully grown.*

Put ½ inch (1 cm) gravel in flowerpot.

Fill pot with soil.

Wet soil thoroughly.

Make shallow furrows.

Plant seeds and cover with soil.

vegetable seeds in pots indoors. They later remove the plants from the pots and plant them in the ground.

A garden that is a little larger than a classroom can provide all the vegetables a family of four will need for a year! After planning vegetables, the gardener must protect them from diseases, insect pests, and rabbits, as well as other small animals.

■ LEARN BY DOING

You can plant a garden in one or more flowerpots, in a window box, or on a small or large area of ground. No matter where you grow plants, the process is the same. Here is how to grow plants in a flowerpot.

The best way to get seeds is to buy a small package. Supermarkets, hardware stores, and garden supply stores are some of the places you can buy seeds in the early spring. If you cannot buy any, you can get seeds from some of the food you eat. Tomatoes, corn, peppers, peas, cantaloupes, watermelons, apples, oranges, and grapefruits are some vegetables and fruits that will supply you with seeds. You must take the seeds from them before cooking.

Put a one-half-inch (about 1 cm) layer of gravel at the bottom of each flowerpot. Fill the pots with soil. Add some peat or fertilizer to enrich the soil. Wet the soil thoroughly. Use a pencil to make shallow furrows (rows) in the soil. Put about ten seeds into the furrows in each pot. (Some seeds may not grow.) Cover the seeds with soil and press the soil down gently. Put the flowerpots into shallow containers, such as soup plates or dessert dishes. Add water to the shallow container whenever the soil feels dry.

When the seeds have sprouted and the plants are about 1½ inches (4 cm) tall, you must make sure that each plant will have room to grow. You will want only one plant in each flowerpot. Choose the healthiest plant and pull all the others out of the soil. This is called *thinning.*

One of the most famous gardens in the United States is the International Peace Garden in the Turtle Mountains of North Dakota. It is a 2,200-acre (890-hectare) area that extends across the border into Canada. The garden commemorates the long friendship between the United States and her neighbor.

▼ *Protecting plants with mulch like grass cuttings keeps the soil moist and controls weeds.*

James Garfield had a party trick in which he wrote Greek with one hand and at the same time wrote Latin with the other.

Be sure that your plants receive the right amount of sunlight. Put the flowerpots where the sun will shine on them as long as possible each day. Buy a container of plant food, and feed the plants according to its directions.

As your plants grow, you must watch them carefully to see that they are not being harmed by insects or disease. To get rid of these attackers, spray or dust the plants with insect and fungus killers, or with a substance recommended by organic gardeners. Weeds may also harm your plants. Remove them as they sprout.

If you have followed all the steps carefully, your plants will be healthy. You will have flowers and vegetables, if you tend your plants carefully and have the patience to wait for them to bloom or ripen.

If you have planted seeds that grow into fruit trees, they will eventually become so big that they can no longer grow in a small flowerpot. They will have to be transplanted into the earth or into large wooden tubs made for holding trees. If you planted orange or grapefruit seeds, you can trans-

plant them outdoors only if you live in Florida or the warmer parts of Texas, Arizona, and California. ■

ALSO READ: FERTILIZER, FLOWER, FLOWER FAMILIES, FUNGUS, GARDEN FLOWERS, INSECTICIDE.

GARFIELD, JAMES A. (1831–1881) In 1865 an angry mob gathered outside a building on Wall Street in New York City. News had just reached the city that President Lincoln had been assassinated. Several speakers tried to calm the crowd without success.

Then Congressman James A. Garfield of Ohio stepped out onto the balcony of the building. "Fellow citizens!" he said in a calm, reassuring voice. "God reigns and the Government in Washington still lives." The crowd was deeply moved. They drifted away. There was no more talk of violence.

The congressman who handled the situation so well was born in a log cabin in Ohio not far from Cleveland. James Garfield was two years old when his father died. As soon as James was old enough, he earned money by doing chores for his neighbors. He found work on a canal boat when he was 17. But James was not satisfied. He worked his way through a school near his home. Then he attended the Ohio school later known as Hiram College. He graduated from Williams College in Massachusetts in 1856 and returned to teach Latin and Greek. He became Hiram College's president.

Garfield fought on the side of the North in the Civil War. He was a brave soldier and was made a major general. In 1863, President Lincoln asked him to quit the Army and run for Congress, because men who knew the Army's problems were needed in Congress. Garfield won the election and served 17 years as a congressman. In 1880, he was elected President.

▼ Garden plants can often be seen at their best in local parks and municipal gardens.

JAMES GARFIELD
TWENTIETH PRESIDENT   MARCH 4–SEPTEMBER 19, 1881

Born: November 19, 1831, Orange, Ohio
Parents: Abram and Eliza Ballou Garfield
Education: Williams College, Williamstown, Massachusetts
Religion: Disciples of Christ
Occupation: Teacher
Political Party: Republican
State Represented: Ohio
Married: 1858, to Lucretia Rudolph (1832–1918)
Children: 2 daughters, 5 sons (1 daughter and 1 son died in childhood)
Died: Elberon, New Jersey, September 19, 1881
Buried: Lake View Cemetery, Cleveland, Ohio

Garfield was a likable, scholarly gentleman. But no one knows what kind of President he would have been. In Garfield's time, even minor officials in the Federal Government were appointed by the President. His first four months in office were spent interviewing job applicants. On July 2, he planned to travel to his 25th college reunion. In the Washington railroad station, he was shot by a man whose application for a job had been turned down. Garfield suffered for more than two months while all over the United States people waited anxiously. He finally died on September 19. His Vice-President, Chester A. Arthur, was sworn into office as President shortly afterward.

After Garfield's death, a shocked public demanded reform in the method of filling many government jobs. Two years later, Congress passed a civil service act, which provided for examinations to decide which men and women were best qualified for these jobs.

ALSO READ: ARTHUR, CHESTER A.; AS-SASSINATION; LINCOLN, ABRAHAM.

GARIBALDI, GIUSEPPE (1807–1882) The patriot who did much to free Italy from foreign rule was Giuseppe Garibaldi, a fisherman's son. As a young man, he joined in a revolt of young Italians who wanted to free the small states of Italy from rule by Austrians, French, and Spanish and unite them into one nation. In 1834, Garibaldi had to flee into exile. He spent some years fighting as a guerrilla in South America, where he had many adventures.

However, he never ceased dreaming of a free Italy. He returned home, and fought for the new Roman Republic against the French and Austrians. Again he had to flee into exile, this time to the United States. In 1854 he came back to Italy. By this time, Count Camillo Cavour and Giuseppe Mazzini, two other Italian patriots, were planning another revolt.

In 1860, Garibaldi led a small army, the "Thousand Volunteers" or "Redshirts," in a landing on Sicily, which he freed from Spanish control. He invaded mainland Italy and captured Naples. This victory helped make possible the uniting of Italy under King Victor Emmanuel. Garibaldi, a longtime republican, handed over his army to the king and retired to live quietly on the island of Caprera. But he returned to the struggle in 1862, trying vainly to take Rome from the Pope. In 1874 he became a member of the Italian parliament. He is remembered as one of his country's greatest heroes.

ALSO READ: ITALY.

In 1850, Garibaldi had to flee to the United States where he worked for a time as a candlemaker on Staten Island, New York.

▼ *The Italian patriot and freedom-fighter Giuseppe Garibaldi.*

GARRICK, DAVID (1717–1779)
David Garrick was one of England's most famous actors. He was known especially for his acting in the plays of William Shakespeare.

Garrick was born in Hereford, England. He liked to recite as a child and developed an early interest in the theater. At age 20 he went to London with his tutor, Samuel Johnson. There he studied law and became a wine merchant, but he finally turned to acting. His greatest parts were the title roles of Shakespeare's *Richard III* and *Hamlet*. His style of acting was different from the usual style. He used broad, dramatic gestures and a voice full of emotion. Today this acting style would be considered overdone, but at that time people thought it was very realistic. He was as successful in comedies as he was in tragedies.

Garrick became a partner in the Drury Lane Theater in London in 1747, and for many years he combined acting with theater-managing. He also helped produce the first Shakespearean festival to be held at Shakespeare's birthplace, Stratford-on-Avon, in 1769.

ALSO READ: ACTORS AND ACTING; DRAMA; JOHNSON, SAMUEL; SHAKESPEARE, WILLIAM.

GAS You know that you could not live without the air that surrounds the Earth. But did you ever *think* about air? You cannot see it, smell it, or taste it, so perhaps you just take it for granted. But air is really a complicated substance, a mixture of more than a dozen chemical substances.

The elements that make up air are gases. Gas is one of the three normal states of matter (the other two are liquid and solid). A substance is a solid if it has a fixed shape and a fixed *volume* (the space a thing takes up). A brick is an example of a solid. You can put a brick into any container and it still holds its shape and takes up the same amount of space.

A substance is a liquid if it has a fixed volume but no fixed shape. You can put some water in a short glass, then pour it into a tall one. Its shape changes as it is moved from container to container. Only its volume stays the same.

A gas has no fixed shape and no fixed volume. A gas takes the shape *and* the volume of whatever container it is put into. Suppose you had a tightly sealed box that had no air in it. You could put rocks into the box until it was half full. But if you tried to half-fill the box with air, you would fail. As you pumped air in, the molecules of the air would spread out—the air would *expand*—to fill the box completely.

A substance is called a gas if it is a gas at ordinary temperatures—between freezing and about 100° F (38° C). Any gas cooled to a low enough temperature will become a liquid. And any liquid heated to a high enough temperature will become a gas. If you take ice cubes from the

At very high temperatures all matter turns into gas. For example, the sun contains no solid or liquid matter. It is a huge ball of very hot gases.

▼ *The famous English actor David Garrick, acting with Mrs. Susannah Cibber in Thomas Otway's tragedy,* Venice Preserv'd, *first produced in 1682.*

freezer and put them in a pot, they will melt. If you heat the water, it will turn to steam—which is a gas.

Of the 92 chemical elements found in nature, only 11 are gases at ordinary temperatures. These are hydrogen, helium, nitrogen, oxygen, fluorine, neon, chlorine, argon, krypton, xenon, and radon. All other gases are compounds made up of two or more elements. For example, the element carbon, a solid, combines with oxygen to form two different gases. One is *carbon dioxide*, which forms when anything containing carbon is burned in the open air or in pure oxygen. The other is *carbon monoxide*. This poisonous gas forms when a carbon-containing substance is burned in a container where only a small amount of oxygen is available. The exhaust from automobile engines contains carbon monoxide.

Gases are made up of molecules. The molecules of a solid are packed very tightly together, and so do not move very much. The molecules of a liquid are not so tightly packed together, and so can move around somewhat. Gas molecules are very far apart from one another, and move very rapidly—several hundred feet a second (100 feet = 30.5 m). But gas molecules constantly crash into each other. An average gas molecule crashes into more than four billion other molecules every second!

If you put gas into a closed container, such as a beach ball, the molecules of gas constantly crash into the walls of the ball. Each collision makes a little push against the ball, and all the pushes together cause *pressure*. You feel the pressure when you squeeze the ball.

Boyle's Law If you take the air from the ball and pump it into another beach ball half the size of the first one, the air must fit into half its original volume. The molecules of gas have less room, so they crash into each other—and into the beach ball—more often. The volume is smaller and the pressure has increased. The ball feels harder.

But, if you pump the air into a ball twice as large as the first ball, the gas molecules have more room in which to travel, so collisions happen less often. As volume increases, pressure decreases. The ball feels softer.

This relationship between volume and pressure was first announced by Robert Boyle, an English chemist, in 1662. It is now called Boyle's Law. Boyle's Law is true as long as the temperature of the gas does not change while its volume changes.

Charles's Law In about 1787, a French scientist named Jacques Charles made another important discovery about gases. He found that when a gas is heated, its molecules move more quickly. So the gas molecules crash into the container walls more often. If the container has flex-

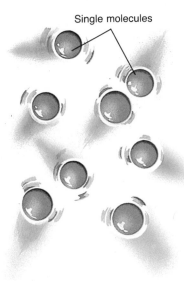

Single molecules

▲ *Why do gases fill any container into which they are put? Because their molecules are not joined together. They move about singly in all directions at great speed. The more molecules there are in the container, the greater the pressure they exert on the walls of the container.*

▼ *A cryogenic storage tank keeps gas in a liquid form by storing it at a low temperature. The liquid hydrogen in this tank is used to fuel the rocket.*

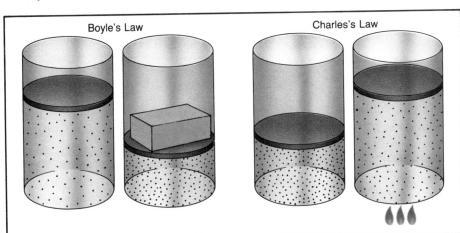

Boyle's Law   Charles's Law

LIQUID HYDROGEN
NO SMOKING

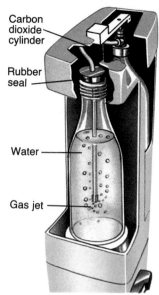

▲ *Carbonated drinks are made by forcing the gas carbon dioxide to dissolve in the drink under pressure. This machine is for home use.*

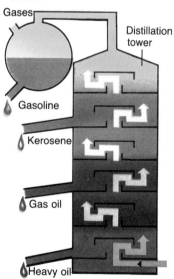

▼ *To get gasoline from oil, the oil has to be distilled. The gasoline vaporizes as the oil is heated, and is collected at the top of the tower. Liquids with higher boiling points, such as kerosene, are collected lower down.*

ible (stretchable) walls, the walls will expand (the volume will increase). If the walls cannot expand, the pressure of the gas increases. The effect of temperature on volume and pressure is usually called Charles's Law. Sometimes it is called Gay-Lussac's Law. Charles did not publish his findings, and in 1802 another French scientist, Joseph Gay-Lussac, independently discovered the law.

■ **LEARN BY DOING**

You can "prove" Charles's Law. You will need a double boiler, an empty soda bottle, and a balloon. Put water in both pots of the double boiler. Pull the balloon over the top of the bottle, and stand the bottle in the top pot of water. Turn the burner on under the double boiler. You can make the balloon expand more quickly by pouring a few drops of water into the soda bottle before you pull the balloon over it. ■

ALSO READ: ATOM, BALLOON, CHEMISTRY, DISTILLATION, ELEMENT, HYDROGEN, LIQUID, MATTER, NITROGEN, OXYGEN, PHYSICS, SOLID.

GASOLINE When a fuel is burned, it produces heat energy. Gasoline is the fuel used to power most automobile engines. It is also used in outboard boat engines, and the engines of motorcycles, motorbikes, snowmobiles, and small airplanes.

Gasoline is a mixture of chemical compounds called *hydrocarbons*. These compounds are composed of the elements hydrogen and carbon.

Most gasoline comes from *petroleum*, which comes from oil wells. This is a very complicated mixture of many different hydrocarbons. Gasoline contains lighter, more flammable hydrocarbons. It is separated from petroleum by a process called *distillation*.

Distillation is done in an oil refinery. The mixture of petroleum is

warmed and the liquid hydrocarbons boil and change to gas. The lighter hydrocarbons boil more easily and separate from the petroleum.

Some other parts of the petroleum can be turned into gasoline. This is done by heating them so that large molecules break into smaller ones. The process is called *cracking*. Usually the vapor is passed over chemicals called *catalysts*. These make it easier to break the molecules. This type of cracking is called *catalytic* cracking, or cat-cracking.

The gasoline that burns in your family's car is not just gasoline. It includes chemicals to make the gas burn more smoothly, to increase mileage, and to keep the engine clean. Lead is often included among these chemicals. But lead in car exhausts is very bad for people, especially children. Now more and more people are using lead-free gasoline.

ALSO READ: AIR POLLUTION, CHEMISTRY, DISTILLATION, ELEMENT, FUEL, NATURAL GAS, PETROLEUM.

GAUGUIN, PAUL (1848–1903) Eugène Henri Paul Gauguin was born in France, but his mother was Peruvian, and he spent part of his boyhood in Lima, Peru. Perhaps the memory of beautiful flowers and golden-skinned people was what took him halfway around the world.

Gauguin did not begin to paint until he was in his mid-twenties, already married and working in a bank. He studied very hard and painted in all his free time. He became friendly with the Impressionists. After ten years, he left his job and family in order to paint.

Looking for tropical scenes to paint, Gauguin sailed to Panama. All his money was soon gone, and he was forced to work as a ditchdigger on the canal France was building across Panama. Gauguin earned enough money to sail to the Caribbean island of

Martinique, but illness forced him to return to France. By then he had developed a very unique style of painting, using vivid colors and strong shapes.

Gauguin returned to the tropics again in a few years—this time to Tahiti in the South Pacific. There he did the famous painting you see here, *Fatata Te Miti*—"by the sea" in the language of Tahiti.

Notice how Gauguin uses broad, curving areas of intense color. Depth is barely suggested by these flat color areas. You get the feeling of a primitive people living in a strange and beautiful civilization. You sense a certain peaceful mood—through color, gestures, and the smooth, rolling rhythms of the lines. Gauguin shows his drawing talent in the roundness of forms, the branches of a tree, and the silhouette of the beach. They give you a feeling of being by the sea. Now look at the picture and see how your eye is directed—diagonally from the foreground to the background, because of the overlapping curves. Look once more and try to see the painting as a decorative design—not as a landscape. Gauguin did many paintings as decorative designs, as did the modern abstract painters who followed him.

After two years, Gauguin took this painting and several others back to France. They caused much excitement among artists, but no one bought them. He returned to Tahiti and lived there the rest of his life.

ALSO READ: IMPRESSIONISM.

GAZETTEER A gazetteer is a geographical dictionary. It is arranged alphabetically just like a normal dictionary.

Geographical names are often spelled differently in different languages. "Roma" in Italian is "Rome" in English. Most gazetteers include all the different spellings of names.

Very often, a gazetteer also shows

▲ Fatata Te Miti, *by Paul Gauguin. This great French painter spent many years in Tahiti, painting the people and events he saw there.*

the pronunciations of all the geographical names. To do this, special symbols—phonetic marks—are shown over the letters, or symbols may even replace the letters. Many gazetteers—like many dictionaries—use the *International Phonetic Alphabet* for this.

A gazetteer usually contains much more than just spellings and pronunciations. It tells where the rivers, lakes, mountains, cities, and villages are located. It sometimes tells how many people live in the cities. It often gives the heights of mountains and the lengths of rivers. It may even give short descriptions of countries and cities, and may tell a little about the history of the country or how the people live.

A gazetteer is included in many atlases. It serves as an index of names in the atlas. Gazetteers are also printed as separate books. The next time you visit the library, look at a gazetteer. See if your town or city is listed.

ALSO READ: ATLAS, REFERENCE BOOK.

GEAR Gears are wheels with raised parts (*teeth*) around their edges. Gears are used to transmit (pass on) power and motion. Many kinds of machines,

It was during a quarrel with Gauguin that the great painter Vincent van Gogh cut off one of his own ears.

1047

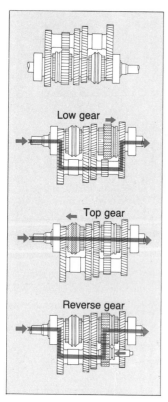

▲ *In an automobile engine, the gearbox carries power from the engine to the mainshaft connected to the wheels, but changes the speed. At low gear, the engine turns the mainshaft at a slower speed. In top gear, the force is transmitted directly through the gearbox, so that the mainshaft turns faster. To reverse, a gear wheel called an idler turns the mainshaft in the opposite direction.*

from watches, clocks, and wind-up toys to cars, planes, and ships, could not move without gears.

An axle passes through the center of each gear. When two gears are placed edge to edge, their teeth fit together. Turning the axle of one gear causes that gear to spin, and it in turn pushes the second gear around, turning that gear's axle, too. A set of two or more gears working together is called a *gear train.*

Gears have two main uses—to increase the power of an engine or to increase its speed. With the correct gear train, a small engine can pull a very heavy load, or a slow-moving engine can operate a high-speed machine. You can see how this works in the drawing below.

In the top gear train in the drawing, a gear with 20 teeth turns a gear with 10 teeth. Each time the *drive* gear—the one with 20 teeth—turns once, the second gear turns twice. But the second gear turns with only half as much power as the first gear. If two units of force turn the drive gear, the second gear produces only one unit of force.

The bottom gear train works the other way around. Each time the drive gear turns once, the second gear—which has twice as many teeth—makes half a turn. But it has twice as much power as the drive gear.

Work is the amount of weight moved times the distance the weight

▲ *Gear wheels in a medieval windmill in Turkey. Gears allow a windmill turning up and over to work a grindstone turning round and round.*

is moved. The top gear train can pull its weight twice as far as the bottom gear train, but the bottom train can pull twice the weight of the top one. So, with the same amount of force applied, both trains do the same amount of work.

Gears have another important job in many machines. They change the direction of a force. Special gears are used to do this. One special gear, the *worm* gear, is shown in the diagram. Automobiles use an arrangement something like this to change the turning force of the steering wheel into the sideways force that turns the wheels. Another gear arrangement changes the turning force of the engine into the rotation of the wheels.

■ LEARN BY DOING

You can buy all sorts of gears and axles at almost any hobby shop. Try setting up several gear trains to see what work they can do. If you added a 40-tooth gear to each gear train in the drawing, what would happen? Where would you put this third gear to get the most use from it? ■

ALSO READ: MACHINE.

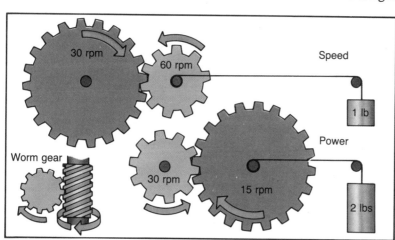

GEHRIG, LOU (1903–1941)

Henry Louis Gehrig was one of the all-time great professional baseball players. He was born in New York City and attended Columbia University. He played first base for the New York Yankees from 1925 to 1939. He was known as "The Iron Horse" because he played 2,130 games in a row.

Gehrig was one of the best hitters in baseball history. He played in seven World Series, won baseball's Most Valuable Player award four times, and was voted into the Baseball Hall of Fame in 1939.

Gehrig suffered from a rare and incurable nerve disease. It is today often called *Lou Gehrig's disease*. In 1939, Gehrig was forced to retire from baseball. He served briefly as a parole commissioner in New York City. Many people mourned his death in 1941 at age 38.

ALSO READ: BASEBALL.

GEIGER COUNTER
The Geiger counter is named after one of its inventors, Hans Geiger (1882–1945), a German physicist. The Geiger counter is used to detect tiny charged

particles. These particles move at such high speeds that they electrify gas molecules. If just one charged particle passes through a Geiger counter, it electrifies the gas in the counter and causes a tiny pulse of electric current to flow. The Geiger counter shows this pulse as a "click." The clicking tells that radioactive material producing charged particles is nearby. Many clicks mean a large quantity of such material. Prospectors use Geiger counters to locate radioactive ores.

A Geiger counter can help find radioactive material that has been lost. A hospital once threw away a tiny but valuable piece of radium by mistake. A Geiger counter was rushed to the city dump where the hospital trash was burned. Workers carried the Geiger counter back and forth for several hours. Suddenly, the counter began to click. The place where it clicked the fastest was shoveled out, and the ashes were sent to a laboratory. The piece of radium was soon found and returned to the hospital.

If people are exposed to radioactive materials, they may become very sick. Geiger counters are used constantly to ensure that the people who work with such materials are safe.

ALSO READ: ATOM, RADIATION, URANIUM.

GEM
A cut and polished stone is called a gem, as long as it has three important qualities: it is unusual or rare, it is beautiful, and it is durable. The stones that are the rarest are called *precious stones*, and these are the most expensive. Tinted diamonds of different colors are very rare and very precious. Another thing that makes a stone precious is its size. Large dia-

◀ Geiger counters are used by prospectors to find deposits of radioactive ores like uranium.

▲ Lou Gehrig, one of the greatest baseball players of all time.

People have always thought that beautiful gems have magical properties. There is a story that in 1534 Pope Clement VII became ill. To cure his sickness he swallowed 40,000 ducats' worth of powdered gems. Of course, this drastic action only hastened the pope's death.

January	February	March	
Garnet	Amethyst	Aquamarine	Bloodstone
Faithfulness	Sincerity	Courage	
April	May	June	Alexandrite
Diamond	Emerald	Pearl	Natural light / Artificial light
Innocence	Love	Health	
July	August	September	
Ruby	Peridot / Sardonyx	Sapphire	
Contentment	Married happiness	Clear thinking	
October	November	December	
Opal / Tourmaline	Topaz / Citrine	Turquoise / Zircon	
Hope	Fidelity	Prosperity	

▲ *Every month of the year has its gemstone—and some have more than one. Do you know your own birthstone? The gems are supposed to bring qualities like love and prosperity to persons' lives.*

The chances of a baby being a girl or a boy are about the same. But one in 16 families with four children has four boys, while another family will have four girls. Much longer strings of boys or girls have been recorded. One French family had nothing but girls—72 of them—in three generations.

monds are more difficult to find than small ones. Garnets are found in beautiful colors and many sizes. But garnets are not as rare as diamonds, so they are called *semiprecious stones*. Other semiprecious stones include the topaz and the amethyst.

Gems are lasting. Diamonds are very hard. Rubies and sapphires are not so hard as diamonds, but they are harder than most other materials. Wealth can be kept in the form of precious stones, and passed on from one generation to another. The famous Hope diamond first appeared about 1830, cut from a larger diamond that was stolen during the French Revolution in 1792.

Not all gems are stones. Pearls are made by oysters and mussels. Amber was once the sap of evergreen trees that lived millions of years ago. Coral is made from skeletons of tiny sea

animals. Jet is a kind of coal.

Birthstones and Synthetics In ancient times a certain gem was supposed to be lucky for a person born under a certain sign of the Zodiac, or with a certain birth date. This is how the idea of birthstones started. The color was more important than the type of stone. Today it is the type of gem that is important. For example, garnet is associated with January and turquoise with December. Many months have several different birthstones. Do you know your birthstone?

Synthetic or artificial gems are produced in industrial laboratories. Emeralds can be made that are very similar to real emeralds. Synthetic diamonds, rubies, sapphires, and other stones can also be made.

ALSO READ: DIAMOND, MINERAL.

GENETICS Do you look like your father or your mother? What makes a child usually look like one parent or the other, but sometimes like neither the father nor the mother? What prevents yellow roses growing from the seeds of red roses? Answers to these questions may be found in the study of genetics.

A child almost always looks like one of his or her parents, grandparents, aunts, or uncles. Through the parents' sex cells, a child gets the shape of the face, the color of hair and eyes, bone structure, and other features that make him or her the person that you see. The characteristics that children inherit from their families make up their *heredity*.

All apples are alike, or similar, in most ways. Yet some apples have red skins, others have yellow skins, and some are green. Some kinds are hard, and some are soft. Some are sweet and others are sour. Differences such as these that are among similar living things are called *variations*.

Genetics is the study of those biological factors that guide heredity and determine variation in fairly similar living things. It is becoming a very important science.

People have always known that in every generation of plants or animals offspring vary in many small ways, but no one knew the reason. People who bred plants and animals knew that now and then an offspring with a distinguishable variation would appear. A Massachusetts farmer, in 1791, had a sheep that gave birth to a lamb with legs much shorter than its parents' legs. The short-legged sheep passed short-leggedness on to its offspring. And from this one short-legged sheep came a new kind of sheep that could not jump fences, as long-legged sheep can. None of the breeders understood why.

Mendel and His Peas In the late 1850's an Austrian monk, Gregor Mendel, began a large number of experiments in growing peas. The pods of some peas were smoothly curved and some were twisted. The coats of the peas were gray, gray-brown, or leather-brown. Some coats were smooth, some wrinkled. Within

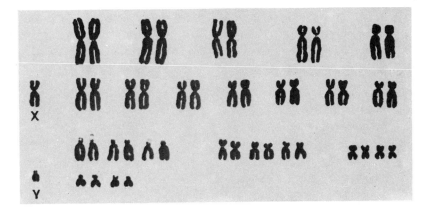

the coats, the peas were green or yellow. Some pea plants were short and some were tall. Mendel kept a careful record of parents and offspring. He found the peas varied in each generation according to a pattern.

Mendel concluded that characteristics of an organism were determined by *factors*, small units in the sex cells of its parents. For each characteristic there were two factors, one from the sperm of the father and one from the egg of the mother. Some factors were *dominant*: they always appeared in the offspring. Others were *recessive*: they did not appear in the offspring unless both parents gave the same recessive factor. Mendel published his laws of heredity in 1865, but they were largely ignored.

De Vries and Mutation However, 35 years after Mendel, a Dutch scientist, Hugo de Vries, did breeding experiments with primroses. He found that now and then a primrose would appear with a large variation, one that seemed to be entirely new. He called this kind of variation a *mutation*, from the Latin word *mutare*, meaning "change." The short legs of the Massachusetts sheep were a mutation. Before publishing his theories,

▲ *The 46 chromosomes from a man, arranged in their 22 pairs, plus the single X and Y chromosomes. Women have no Y chromosomes. Both men and women may have more than one X chromosome, and a very few men have more than one Y chromosome.*

A recently developed branch of genetics is called *genetic engineering*. Scientists working in this field believe that soon they will be able to "breed" wholesome foods. They believe also that, in the future, it may be possible to control certain genes that cause hereditary (inherited) diseases.

◄ *Sometimes a fertilized egg divides to form two separate embryos, each of which becomes a baby. These twins have the same genetic make-up, and are identical. Unlike twins occur when two eggs are fertilized.*

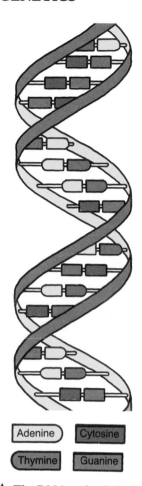

Adenine Cytosine
Thymine Guanine

▲ *The DNA molecule is a very long double helix (spiral). The two strands interlock with each other. Each of the four units of which the strand is made up can interlock with only one other.*

De Vries checked to see what had been written on the subject. To his astonishment, he discovered that Mendel had done it all before him!

Genes Meanwhile, many scientists had been working to understand the way living cells reproduce. They found that, in reproduction, the important part of the cell is the *nucleus*. They also found that within the nucleus are threadlike objects that line up in the shape of rods, just before a cell divides. These objects were named *chromosomes*. Almost every cell of the human body has two similar sets of 23 chromosomes each. The exceptions are the sex cells. The male sex cell, the *sperm*, has one set of 23 chromosomes, and the female sex cell, the egg, has one set of 23 chromosomes.

With the discovery of chromosomes and the rediscovery of Mendel's work, scientists understood that the factors causing resemblances and variations to pass from one generation to the next are in the chromosomes. They named these unknown factors *genes*.

By the end of the first half of the 20th century, scientists discovered that a chromosome is made up of hundreds of genes. Each gene has a definite place in a chromosome.

Chemists proved that genes form part of giant molecules. In 1944, a U.S. chemist, Oswald T. Avery, discovered that the key material of heredity is *deoxyribonucleic acid*, or DNA. In 1953, Francis H. C. Crick of Britain and James D. Watson of the United States worked out the chemical structure of DNA.

DNA and Heredity Crick and Watson discovered that DNA is shaped like a double *helix* (spiral), with chemical cross rungs similar to those of a ladder. Each ladder is made up of a number of compounds.

When a sperm unites with an egg, the egg divides into two cells. The new cells divide, and eventually there may be billions of cells making up a complete plant or animal.

When any cell is about to divide, the DNA molecule divides too. One of the most important facts about DNA is that it can divide into two, producing two "daughter" molecules of DNA that are identical to the "parent." This process of division is called *replication*. During replication the DNA ladder unwinds and splits into two, down the middle of the rungs. Then each half-ladder forms itself into a complete ladder with the help of special enzymes in the cell. As they are constructed, the ladders twist into the characteristic spiral form. This whole process involves the hundreds of genes of each chromosome, thousands in each cell. When the DNA has doubled, the chromosomes split in half, and so does the rest of the cell. Two new cells are formed. Each new cell has a new, whole set of chromosomes.

Sometimes during the formation of sex cells, something goes wrong. The DNA does not reproduce itself exactly as it was in either of the parents'

◄ *James Watson (left) and Francis Crick, who won the Nobel Prize in 1962 for their work in establishing the structure of the DNA molecule.*

BROWN EYES OR BLUE?

1   2   3   4

Why are your eyes the color they are? It is because of your parents' genes. If both of your parents have two blue-eye genes, all their children will have blue eyes (1). If one parent has two brown-eye genes and the other has two blue-eye genes, all the children will have brown eyes because the brown-eye gene is *dominant* (2). But those children will have a *recessive* blue-eye gene: if they have children with a blue-eyed person (3), or with another person who has a recessive blue-eye gene (4), some of those children may have blue eyes.

cells. As a result, a new gene is formed. A new gene means a new characteristic, a new variation. The plant or animal that develops from such cells is called a mutant. Scientists have learned that heat, chemicals, and X rays can change the genetic code and cause mutations.

By understanding the genetic code, scientists are close to discovering how life began on Earth, how the millions of kinds of plants came to be, and how different animals developed over the centuries.

Genetic Engineering In recent years scientists have been experimenting with bacteria and yeasts (a type of fungus) to produce new foods and new medicines—substances that cannot be made by normal chemistry. Scientists take one type of DNA and put it into a bacterium or yeast-cell. The bacterium or yeast-cell begins to reproduce the "new" type of DNA. Soon large quantities of the desired substance are produced.

ALSO READ: BIOCHEMISTRY, CELL, CHEMISTRY, EARTH HISTORY, EVOLUTION, FLOWER, PLANT BREEDING.

GENGHIS KHAN (1162–1227) Genghis Khan was born near the shores of Lake Baikal, north of the Gobi Desert in Siberia. His real name was Temujin. His father was chief, or *khan*, of a small Mongol tribe. Temujin was 13 years old when his father died. Temujin became the chief of his tribe. He proved himself a military genius and soon became master of all the Mongol tribes that lived in Siberia. He was then called Genghis Khan, which means "greatest of all rulers."

Genghis Khan turned the Mongol

▶ *Genghis Khan, the greatest of all Mongol leaders. He owed his conquests largely to the fact that his soldiers were the finest cavalry of the time. Kahn was also skilled in strategic and tactical warfare.*

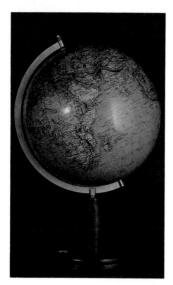

▲ *A modern globe on a stand. Only a globe can show the Earth's surface as it really is. A flat map distorts the shape of the Earth's surface.*

The geographic center of the United States (48 states) is near Lebanon, Smith County, Kansas. Its position is latitude 39°50′ N, longitude 98°35′ W.

▶ *A photograph of Earth taken from an artificial satellite. Clouds cover much of the surface. The color wheel (upper center) lets scientists check the real colors of the Earth.*

tribes into a great army. This army first conquered all of China. It then invaded and conquered the land that now forms Iran, Turkey, northern India, and Russia. The Mongols never took prisoners but killed all who fought against them and destroyed entire cities. All of Europe was terrified of the Mongols, but they never invaded Western Europe.

ALSO READ: MONGOLIA, RUSSIAN HISTORY.

GEOGRAPHY What conditions help oranges grow in California? Through what countries does the Nile River flow? What kinds of houses are built by the people who live on islands in the South Pacific Ocean? Why do landscapes look the way they do? These are questions that geography answers.

Geography is the study of our planet as the home of human beings. It describes the surface features of the Earth and their distribution. *Geographers* do not try to explain, for example, how the Rocky Mountains were formed. That is a job for geologists. Geographers study the height of each mountain, the location of valleys, what rivers flow from the Rockies, and what towns and roads are in the mountain region. They show how the Rockies have come to look the way they do today. They also explain that the Rocky Mountains guard the west

▲ *Geographers study many different types of landforms. This landform is a river delta on the island of Haiti. Many plants grow in delta areas.*

coast from cold winds and give California a warm climate for oranges to grow in. Maps are important tools of geographers. Mapmakers are called *cartographers*.

Geography may be divided into two main branches—physical geography and human geography. *Physical geography* describes and studies the surface features of the Earth—oceans, continents, mountains, hills, rivers, lakes, gulfs, bays, and many other land and water features. Physical geographers make maps showing where metal ores, coal, oil, and natural gas are located. They also map the climates of the world. *Biogeography* is the study of where on Earth particular plants and animals are found.

Human geography describes and studies what human beings do in and on land and water. This wide subject links the Earth sciences with the social sciences, and it has several branches. *Political geography* deals with the boundaries of countries and the effects of human political activities on geographic features. *Economic geography* studies the natural resources of an area and the ways in which people have made use of them. The crops it grows, the minerals and fuels extracted from it, its industries, its methods of transportation—all are important aspects of an area's economic geography.

Human geography divides the peoples of the world into groups called *cultures*. The people of a culture share many things, including what they look like, how they dress, earn their living, marry, raise children, and what foods they grow and eat. Human geographers share the work of studying these cultures with anthropologists and sociologists.

ALSO READ: ANTHROPOLOGY, CONTINENT, CULTURE, GEOLOGY, LAKE, MAP, MOUNTAIN, OCEAN, RIVER, SOCIOLOGY.

GEOLOGIC TIME see EARTH HISTORY.

GEOLOGY Have you ever wondered how mountains, lakes, rivers, oceans, and other physical features of the Earth were formed? Have you ever wondered if these parts of the Earth always looked as they do today? The science of geology deals with questions such as these. The word "geology" comes from two Greek words meaning "Earth study."

Geology includes the study of the substances that make up the Earth, the changes the Earth undergoes, the forces that cause these changes, and the long-dead plants and animals that once lived on Earth. The many branches of geology are normally divided into physical geology and historical geology.

Physical geology is the study of the substances that make up the Earth and of the *processes* that affect either our planet as a whole or local areas of it. Physical geology has many links with physical geography.

Historical geology is the study of the

Earth's history. A historical geologist says that the Rocky Mountains are higher and more rugged than the Appalachian Mountains because the Rockies are thought to be 200 million years "younger" than the Appalachians. The Appalachians are so old that water and wind have worn away all the roughness.

In the table on this page, you can see some of the special kinds of work that geologists do.

How Geology Developed People have puzzled over the appearance of the Earth's surface for thousands of years. They watched storms wash away beaches and ocean currents build sandbars. They felt earthquakes and saw huge rocks shattered by the vibrations. They saw volcanoes appear and shoot fire and ash into the sky. They saw rivers of fiery lava cool into rock. Ancient people made some good guesses about the things they saw happening to the Earth.

Thales, a Greek who lived more than 500 years before Christ, watched mud pile up at the mouth of the Nile River. He also saw ocean waves "eat" away parts of Egypt's shoreline. From these observations, Thales concluded that water changes the Earth's surface by wearing away and building up land areas. Modern geologists agree with Thales.

About 100 years after Thales, Herodotus, another Greek, said that the seashells he found in many parts of Egypt meant that much of that country had once been covered by ocean. Modern geologists agree with Herodotus, too.

Other ancient Greeks and Romans also made interesting geological discoveries. But after the western Roman Empire fell in A.D. 476, people ignored geology for nearly 1,000 years. The basic ideas of modern geology developed slowly during the 1400's, 1500's, and 1600's. The first modern geologist is sometimes said to have been Georg Bauer (1494–1555),

---

MAJOR FIELDS OF GEOLOGY

EARTH HISTORY AND FOSSILS
Historical Geology: History of the Earth through discovering the ages of rock *strata* (layers) and examining their rocks
Paleontology: Fossils of ancient plant and animal life

CHANGES IN THE EARTH'S SURFACE
Structural Geology: Bending and breaking of rocks by natural forces
Geomorphology: Shaping and wearing away of landforms by natural processes, such as erosion

ROCKS AND MINERALS
Petrology: Rocks
Mineralogy: Minerals
Economic Geology: Useful mineral veins and deposits, such as oil and coal

GEOPHYSICS
Meteorology: Atmosphere and causes of weather
Oceanology: Waves, tides, the ocean floor, midocean ridges, deep-sea trenches
Seismology: Earthquakes
Volcanology: Volcanoes
Plate Tectonics: The very major changes of the Earth as the plates of the planet's crust move relative to each other; study of plate tectonics involves oceanology, seismology, volcanology
Planetary Geology: The geophysics of other planets

▼ *Geologists use special tools to examine the rocks and minerals that make up the Earth. Work in the field is vital to geologists.*

▲ *The Badlands of South Dakota are made up of rock strata (layers), which can be clearly seen in this picture.*

▼ *The Colorado Desert has layers of rock that have formed over a period of about 16 million years. The Colorado River and its tributaries have sliced through these layers in the Grand Canyon and other nearby canyons.*

a German who used the Latin name Georgius Agricola. He wrote books on fossils, minerals, and metals. Agricola was the first to group minerals scientifically.

During the 1700's, geologists spent much time arguing about how rocks were formed. One group said the whole world was once covered by a vast ocean. They believed chemicals in the water fell slowly to the bottom of the ocean, where they combined into rocks. These geologists thought that all the changes on the Earth's surface had happened while this ocean covered the world, and that no other changes could ever occur.

Another group of scientists was led by James Hutton, a doctor from Scotland. They said that all rocks formed originally from volcanic lava. More important, these scientists believed that the Earth is always going through very slow changes, and that the study of the changes that were taking place during their lifetime could help people understand what had happened in the past. The ideas of Hutton and his followers form the central ideas of modern geology.

How Geologists Work Geologists do much of their work outdoors. The places where geologists work depend on what they want to study. A *meteorologist* (a scientist who studies weather) who wants to know about hurricanes must work where hurricanes occur—in the Atlantic Ocean or the Caribbean Sea.

A *paleontologist* (a scientist who studies fossils) usually works in areas where he or she can expect to find *fossils* (remains of long-dead animals or plants), such as tar and gravel pits, or where there are rocks that formed from mud at the bottoms of prehistoric rivers and lakes. When paleontologists find a fossil, they take a chunk of rock containing the fossil back to their laboratory. Then they very painstakingly chip and brush the rock away to free the fossil. If the fossil happens to be the many bones of a large animal, they may spend months—or even years—carefully rebuilding the skeleton.

Geophysicists study the Earth as a whole. For example, they study its interior. They use special instruments to study how the shockwaves of earthquakes move through different layers of the Earth. From the way these shockwaves behave, geophysicists can tell much about what the interior of the Earth is like.

Certain geologists study water bodies and the land under them. An

oceanologist is interested in the oceans and seas. A *limnologist* has many similar problems, but these problems are related to fresh inland bodies of water, such as lakes and ponds.

Some land areas of the world are especially interesting to geologists. The Grand Canyon is such a place. The canyon was cut into the rock by the power of the Colorado River. The walls of the canyon are made up of many layers (*strata*) of rock. The oldest layers are at the bottom of the canyon, and the newest layers are at the top. By "reading" the story of the rock strata, geologists can tell much about the history of the Earth.

Many geologists work for industry. They lead the hunt to discover deposits of iron, copper, silver, gold, and other valuable minerals. Geologists also search for pockets of coal, petroleum, natural gas, uranium, and so on. Geologists help plan how to dig a mine or drill an oil well.

Some geologists study rocks or minerals. Through careful work, these scientists have learned what substances make up rocks and minerals and, sometimes, how to take useful or important substances out of the rocks or minerals. By slow, gentle

▼ *The geologist Harrison Schmitt was the first scientist to visit the moon. He took part in the last mission of the Apollo project, in December 1972.*

grinding, geologists can wear a rock so thin that they can see through it with a microscope.

With the beginning of space travel, geologists have turned some of their attention to other planets. Pieces of rocks from the moon have already been studied, and samples from Mars have been tested by "remote control" in the Viking project of 1976. From photographs taken by spacecraft, scientists can tell much about the "geology" of other planets. This field of study, *planetary geology*, is a very exciting one.

For further information on:
Earth History, *see* CONTINENTAL DRIFT, DINOSAUR, EARTH HISTORY, PLATE TECTONICS, ICE AGE.
Things Geologists Study, *see* COAL, EARTHQUAKE, EROSION, FOSSIL, METAL, MINERAL, PALEONTOLOGY, PETROLEUM, ROCK, VOLCANO.
Types of Physical Features, *see* CANYON, CAVE, CONTINENT, DESERT, EARTH, GRAND CANYON, ISLAND, LAKE, MOUNTAIN, OCEAN, VOLCANO, WATERFALL.

GEOMETRY Nature is full of interesting shapes and figures. The design of a flower, the sharp angles and flat surfaces of a snowflake, and the spreading circles of ripples in a lake are all examples of shapes, forms, and figures in nature. Geometry is the study of different kinds of figures and their properties. It also has to do with how shapes, angles, and distances are related. Because geometry is so closely tied to nature, it is one of the oldest branches of mathematics.

The ancient Egyptians discovered geometrical properties quite early. Every year the Nile River overflowed its banks and flooded the countryside. The Egyptians learned to use angles to set up land boundaries that had been washed away. But the Egyptians gained their knowledge of geometry through trial and error. It was the

▲ *Two diver geologists surveying an underwater site. The waterproof instruments they carry enable them to make notes underwater.*

For a long time, people have tried to work out the age of the Earth. In the 1600's, an Irish archbishop named Ussher decided from reading the Scriptures that the world was created in 4004 B.C. This date was for some time printed in the margin of Bibles as the date of the creation. It was not long, however, before geologists realized by examining the rocks that this date was very wrong. We now know that the Earth was formed about 4,600 million years ago.

GEOMETRY

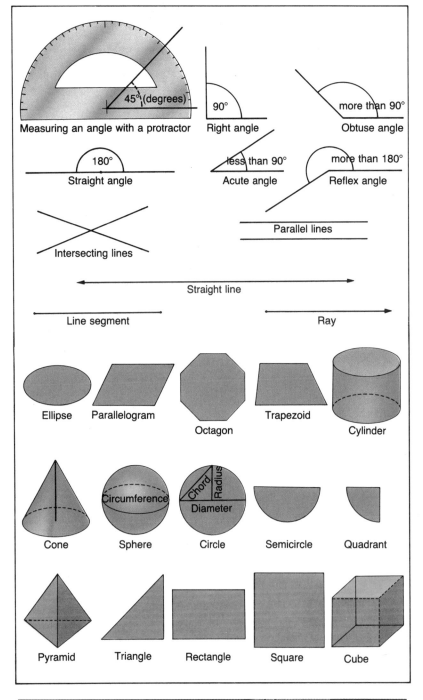

Measuring an angle with a protractor — 45° (degrees)

Right angle — 90°

Obtuse angle — more than 90°

Straight angle — 180°

Acute angle — less than 90°

Reflex angle — more than 180°

Intersecting lines

Parallel lines

Straight line

Line segment

Ray

Ellipse | Parallelogram | Octagon | Trapezoid | Cylinder

Cone | Sphere (Circumference) | Circle (Chord, Radius, Diameter) | Semicircle | Quadrant

Pyramid | Triangle | Rectangle | Square | Cube

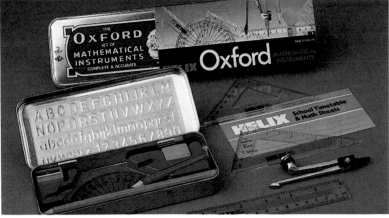

ancient Greeks who first discovered how to work out the properties of shapes and figures by logical reasoning.

The most important person in the early history of geometry was Euclid, a Greek who lived about 300 B.C. in Alexandria, Egypt. He wrote a book about geometry, called *Elements*. In it, he used logic to *prove* that the statements he made about shapes and figures were true. *Elements* is one of the most important books in the history of mathematics and proofs from it are still used today.

Since Euclid's time, many new properties of figures have been discovered, and today the study of geometry is offered in most schools. Geometry is one of the most important branches of mathematics.

The Objects of Geometry Thousands of different shapes exist in the world. In geometry, some are more important than others. The pictures show and name the most important shapes. Study the pictures as you read.

The simplest kind of geometry is *plane geometry*. In it, all the figures are flat and lie in a plane. A *plane* is a flat surface—like a tabletop—only a plane has no thickness. You will never see a plane, but mathematicians find it helpful to imagine them. Mathematicians substitute a piece of paper for a "real" plane.

A *point* is the simplest geometric object. Mathematicians use a dot to show a point, but a point really has no size at all. It is used to locate a position and is thought of as the intersection (meeting) of two lines. A *line* is an important object in geometry. A line has only length—no thickness or width at all. A mark made by a pencil is a good symbol for an actual line.

There are several different kinds of lines. One of the most important is

◀ *A set of geometrical instruments usually includes setsquares (triangles), compasses, and protractors.*

the *straight line*. If you draw a line using a ruler, it is a straight line. It does not curve to the right or left. Most lines are of definite lengths—that is, they have *end points*. If a line has end points, it is called a *line segment*. Sometimes, however, it is helpful to think of the line going on indefinitely. In the picture, the arrows at the end of the line mean that the line goes on and on. A *ray* is a line that has only one end point, and that keeps going in the other direction.

If a line is not straight, it is called a *curved line*. One of the most important curved lines is a *circle*. You can use a *compass* to draw a picture of a circle. A geometric compass does not tell directions. It has two arms, one with a very sharp point, and one with a pencil or pen attached to it. If you hold the sharp end steady and move the pencil end around it, you can draw a circle. The sharp end rests on the *center* of the circle, and the pencil draws a circle around it.

Figures from Lines Plane geometrical figures are made from lines and line segments. Flat figures whose sides are all straight lines are called *polygons*, which comes from a Greek word meaning "figure with many angles." Polygons are named by the number of sides they have. The simplest polygon is a *triangle*, which has three sides. The diagrams show some

polygons and their names. The point where the sides of a polygon intersect to form an angle is called a *vertex*. One of the interesting properties of polygons is that they always have just as many vertices as they have sides.

■ LEARN BY DOING

An important subject of geometry is to study the relationships between the sides, angles, and areas of polygons. You can discover a property of the angles of a triangle.

You will need to have a protractor, which is used to measure angles. The base of the protractor lies along one line of an angle, with the center of the base on top of the vertex of the angle. The number of degrees in the angle is shown by where the other arm of the angle crosses the protractor. Draw several angles and measure them for practice.

Now get a large sheet of paper and draw three or four triangles on it. Letter each vertex (A,B,C, and so on) and measure its angle. Write down the number of degrees of each angle. Finally, for each triangle, add up the number of degrees in each of its angles to get a total for each triangle. Compare the totals. If you have been careful, you will find that each triangle has exactly the same total number of degrees. What is that total? This is one basic rule of geometry—the angles in a triangle add up to 180°. ■

▲ *Geometric shapes can be found in things you see every day. Study this photograph. Can you find a triangle? What other geometric shapes do you see?*

Euclid, the man who made geometry into a science, was very interested in numbers that he called "perfect" numbers. Six is a perfect number because the only numbers that divide exactly into 6 are 1, 2, and 3. And when you add 1, 2, and 3 together they make 6. The next perfect number is 28. The "factors" of 28 are 1, 2, 4, 7, and 14—they all divide exactly into 28. Add them together and you get 28. The next two perfect numbers after 28 are 496 and 8,128. It was not until 1,400 years after Euclid died that the fifth perfect number was found. It is 33,550,336. The sixth one is 8,589,869,056. We do not have enough space to give you the latest perfect number!

George I hated his son, who succeeded him as George II, and they supported rival political factions. George II in turn labeled his son, Frederick, Prince of Wales, and they quarreled over how much money Frederick should be given as an allowance. Frederick died before his father. It was Frederick's son who became George III.

▼ *George II, King of Britain, was a patron of the arts. The most famous person whom he helped was the composer Handel.*

Uses of Geometry Geometry is one of the most useful of all the branches of mathematics. Carpenters, engineers, architects, and designers all need to know geometry so that the things they build will look pleasing and will function properly. Navigators in ships and airplanes use geometry to guide them across long distances. Artists use geometry to make their two-dimensional paintings look real. Surveyors marking the boundaries of property use geometry. Everywhere that shapes and lines are important, geometry is used.

Astronomers use a different type of geometry, *spherical geometry*. They consider geometry not on a plane but on the surface of a sphere. The rules are different. For example, every triangle drawn on a sphere has curved sides and its angles always add up to more than 180°!

ALSO READ: ANGLE, DIMENSION, EUCLID, MATHEMATICS, PYTHAGORAS, RELATIVITY, SURVEYING, SYMMETRY.

GEORGE, KINGS OF GREAT BRITAIN

Great Britain has had six kings named George.

George I (1660–1727) became king of Great Britain in 1714, after the death of his cousin, Queen Anne. He was brought up in Germany, where he was a member of the ruling family of Hanover. George was a Protestant. He spoke only German and was not very popular with the British people. A rebellion by the Jacobites was planned to put the Catholic son of James II (an earlier British king) on the throne in place of George. It failed in 1715. George spent much of his time in Germany and let his ministers run the British government. Parliament (which is something like the United States Congress) gained much power while he was king.

George II (1683–1760) was the son of George I. He became king in 1727. George II was a very brave soldier.

▲ *George III, the king whom many British people blamed for the problems that lost them the North American colonies.*

When Britain went to war with France, he personally commanded his army in a great victory at the Battle of Dettingen in 1743—the last time a British monarch led troops on the battlefield. As king, George usually followed the advice of his wife, Queen Caroline, and his chief ministers, notably Sir Robert Walpole. He suppressed the last rebellion of the Jacobites in 1745 and 1746.

George III (1738–1820) became king in 1760. He was the son of Frederick Louis, Prince of Wales, and the grandson of George II. He was king during the American Revolution, when the United States won its freedom from Great Britain. In 1788, George had the first of several mental breakdowns. Parliament voted to have his son rule in his place as regent, but George soon recovered. Then he again became mentally ill, and in 1811 he was declared insane. Doctors now think he suffered from a disease called porphyria. His son, later George IV, was regent for the nine years before George III's death.

George IV (1762–1830) was a weak and unpopular ruler. He became king in 1820. He had expensive habits and ran up huge debts. Much of his money was spent on building the Chinese-style Pavilion at Brighton and in decorating his houses with furniture and works of art.

George V (1865–1936) was the son of Edward VII and grandson of Queen Victoria. He joined the British navy as a young man and loved the sea. He came to the throne in 1910. King George, his wife Queen Mary, and his family set an example of courage during the long, hard years of World War I. They were much loved by the people. When George died, he was succeeded by his eldest son, Edward VIII.

George VI (1895–1952) served in the navy during World War I. He became king in 1936 when his brother, Edward VIII, gave up the throne. He and his family again helped raise the nation's spirit during the air raids on Britain in World War II. George VI's elder daughter became Queen Elizabeth II.

ALSO READ: ANNE; EDWARD, KINGS OF ENGLAND; ELIZABETH II; ENGLISH HISTORY; JAMES, KINGS OF ENGLAND; VICTORIA.

GEORGIA The name "Savannah" is important in the state of Georgia. There is the Savannah River, 314 miles (505 km) long, which forms most of the state border between Georgia and South Carolina. The river's mouth on the Atlantic Ocean makes a good harbor for oceangoing ships.

The Savannah Indians farmed and hunted on the coastal plain of Georgia before European settlers came to North America. Each village had a temple on a large mound built of earth and shells. The Indians made handsome colored bowls.

The city of Savannah is Georgia's oldest city. It is located on the Savannah River near its mouth. Today, Savannah is the state's third largest city and its chief port. It is noted for its beautiful, wide, shaded streets and many parks. Magnolias, pines, and oaks are found everywhere in Savannah. Many charming, old brick build-

ings and houses dating from the 18th century still stand.

A ship named the *Savannah* tested steam power on the ocean in 1819. It sailed across the Atlantic Ocean from Savannah to England in about four weeks. Its coal supply was small, so steam turned its paddlewheels for only a few days. Sails took the ship most of the way. But the test was worth making.

Finally, *Savannah* is the name of the first atomic-powered cargo ship. It first went to sea in 1962. Its home port is Savannah.

You can see why the name "Savannah" is so important in Georgia's history. But the state has much else to be proud of, too.

The Land and Climate Georgia has a larger area than any other state east of the Mississippi River. This state is in the South. North of it are Tennessee, North Carolina, and South Carolina. To the south lies Florida. Alabama forms its western border.

More than half the state is in the Atlantic coastal plain. This region is rather flat. The southeastern part of the plain features Okefenokee Swamp, where wild ducks, marsh hens, muskrats, opossums, wildcats, and alligators live. Part of the swamp has been made a wildlife refuge.

The land gets higher toward the north. The hilly region called the Piedmont has broad, rounded ridges that form the walls of long valleys.

▲ *George V delivering his Christmas broadcast to the people of the United Kingdom. He was the first British monarch to make such a broadcast. The tradition has continued to this day.*

> In 1943, Georgia became the first state to allow 18-year-olds to vote.

◄ *An old home located at Stone Mountain, near Atlanta, Georgia. It was one of the luxurious plantation mansions built before the Civil War.*

GEORGIA

► *Okefenokee Wildlife Refuge in southeast Georgia is a sanctuary for bears, deer, birds, and alligators.*

The most famous annual event in Georgia is the Masters Golf Tournament held at the Augusta National Golf Course. The world's top golfers compete in the tournament.

Here and there, a single peak stands alone in the Piedmont. One is the famous Stone Mountain near Atlanta. Giant figures have been carved into its steep granite side. They represent three Confederate leaders in the Civil War—Jefferson Davis, Robert E. Lee, and Stonewall Jackson. The northernmost part of Georgia is in the Appalachian Mountains. The Blue Ridge is the main range of these mountains.

The higher sections of Georgia are cooler in summer than the coastal plain. They are colder in winter, too. Most of the state has warm, fairly wet summers and mild winters. Such a climate is good for crops that need plenty of sunshine and rain. Rice and cotton are among these crops. So is indigo, from which dye used to be made. All three were leading crops during Georgia's early history.

History Georgia was the youngest of the English colonies that formed the 13 original United States. The colony of Virginia was more than 100 years old when Georgia was founded.

General James Edward Oglethorpe led the movement to found the colony. He wanted to give poor people in Britain a chance to start new lives in the New World. The British king George II was glad to provide land south of South Carolina. That rich colony was in danger of attack by Spaniards in Florida. A British colony north of Florida would hold the Spaniards back.

The colony was named for the king, and General Oglethorpe was made its first governor. Careful planning was done to make the colony a good one. No settler was to have slaves. Each man was to be given 50 acres (20 hectares) of land. He would grow his own food. To earn money, he would raise silkworms, olives, and wine grapes to trade with Britain.

Early in 1733, General Oglethorpe landed where Savannah is today. He had picked Yamacraw Bluff, a cliff overlooking the Savannah River, as the place for the first settlement. Oglethorpe at once made friends with the Creek Indians who had a village nearby.

But the settlers became discontented as the settlement grew. They wanted to raise indigo and rice on big plantations. They did not want to do the hard work of raising these crops in hot, wet fields. They wanted slaves, so they could raise large crops and make money. The laws were changed, and slavery was allowed in Georgia. Cotton became Georgia's leading crop after the American Revolution. The plantations then needed even more slaves.

Slavery hurt Georgia as it did the other Southern states. Not only the enslaved blacks suffered. Most white settlers owned neither plantations nor slaves. They often could not earn a living because so much of the state's work was done by unpaid black slaves.

The Civil War ended slavery. But it left much of Georgia and many of its cities in ruins. And the problems caused by slavery remained. Blacks could get jobs only as laborers, so they earned very little. White workers earned more than before the Civil

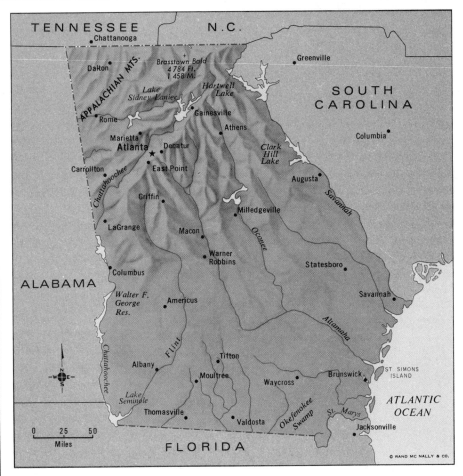

GEORGIA

Capital and largest city
Atlanta (426,000 people)

Area
58,876 square miles (152,488 sq. km).
Rank: 21st

Population
5,976,000 (1985 estimate)
Rank: 13th

Statehood
January 2, 1788 (Fourth of the original thirteen states to ratify the Constitution)

Principal river
Altamaha River (Formed by the joining of the Oconee and Ocmulgee rivers)

Highest point
Brasstown Bald Mountain; 4,784 feet (1,458 m)

Famous people
James Bowie, Erskine Caldwell, President Jimmy Carter, Joel Chandler Harris, Martin Luther King Jr., Sidney Lanier, Margaret Mitchell

STATE EMBLEMS

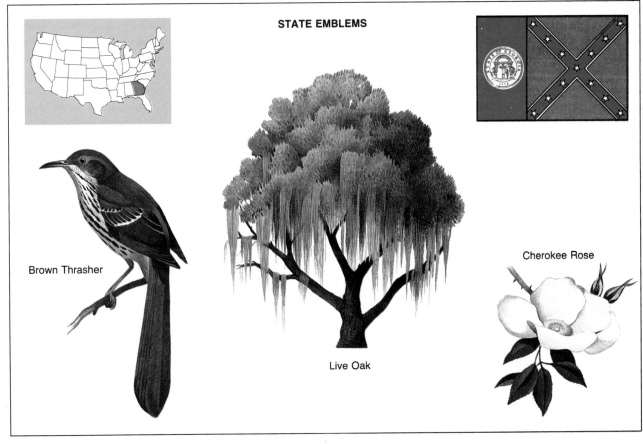

Brown Thrasher

Live Oak

Cherokee Rose

▲ *The impressive cityscape of Atlanta, Georgia.*

War, but not enough to live well. Worst of all, many white people—as in other states—were cruel and unfair to blacks.

But times are changing. Georgia is today fighting poverty, and blacks and whites are working together to solve social, economic, and political problems. Jimmy Carter, governor from 1970 to 1974, encouraged integration of blacks and whites. In 1976, he became the first man from the Deep South to be elected President of the United States since the Civil War.

Georgians At Work Manufacturing is Georgia's biggest business today. Textiles—especially cotton cloth—are the leading products. Transportation equipment and food products are also important, and so are paper products. Every year thousands of pines are cut in Georgia for making paper. Atlanta is the largest manufacturing center in the state. Columbus, Macon, and Savannah have numerous factories.

Agriculture, Georgia's oldest business, is still important. Livestock products (chickens, eggs, cattle, and hogs) earn more money than crops do. Leading crops are peanuts, pecans, soybeans, cotton, and tobacco.

Tourism brings the state nearly twice as much money as agriculture earns. Some visitors go to the beauti-

ful mountains in the north. Others go to the Sea Islands on the coast. Still others visit places where history was made. Spring is a good time to see central Georgia, because the peach orchards near Macon are pink with blossoms. If you would rather see the fruit, go to Macon in midsummer.

ALSO READ: CIVIL RIGHTS, CIVIL WAR, SLAVERY, STATE GOVERNMENT, STATE SYMBOLS.

GERMAN HISTORY Today Germany is divided into two countries, the Federal Republic of Germany, or West Germany, and the German Democratic Republic, or East Germany. This division has existed since 1945. But this is not the first time that Germany has been divided. It did not exist as a single country under a single leader until 1871.

Formation of the Holy Roman Empire Almost 2,000 years ago, the region that is now Germany and France was occupied by wandering tribes called the Germani. When Julius Caesar began his conquest of Gaul in 58 B.C., he encountered these tribes. Within three years, Caesar forced most of the Germani across the Rhine River to their original home, Germania. After several more clashes with the Romans which continued until A.D. 9, the Germani again managed to regain some land on the western bank of the Rhine. The Roman Empire and the Germani, both having strongly defended borders, had generally peaceful relations during the first and second centuries A.D. These 200 relatively peaceful years were of great importance. The Germanic tribes began to group into nations. Included among them were the Goths, Lombards, Vandals, Saxons, and Franks.

With the decline of Roman power in the fifth century A.D., some of these tribal groups again overran Roman

▼ *Martin Luther, an important figure in German history. He was the monk who led the Protestant split from the Roman Catholic Church.*

territory. The kingdom of the Franks became the Frankish Empire, which included most of present-day France and Germany. The greatest of all the Frankish emperors was Charlemagne. After his death in A.D. 814, the empire was divided among his three grandsons. The western portion eventually became modern-day France. The eastern portion, which eventually became modern-day Germany, was ruled by Louis II. But neither Louis, his son Charles "the Fat," nor any of the other leaders who succeeded them could keep Germany united for any long period. Tribal chieftains continued to have absolute control of their lands. Other tribes, especially the Hungarian Magyars, threatened to overrun the country. One German king, Otto I, successfully invaded Italy in A.D. 962 and joined Italy with Germany. He became the first German Holy Roman Emperor. But, like all the other "united" Germanies, this union eventually collapsed. Germany was the scene of immense turmoil for several centuries.

The Reformation   By the end of the Middle Ages, many of the German people were unhappy with the power and bad practices of some Catholic Church leaders in Rome and Germany. Many people hoped for changes in the Church. Great groups of Germans supported Martin Luther when he began to challenge the Church in 1517. This was the beginning of the *Protestant Reformation*, an era in which many changes in religion took place. People who disagreed with the Catholic Church became known as Protestants.

The two religious groups could not live peacefully with one another. This conflict eventually involved all the Protestant and Catholic states of Germany. Some of the best known of these states were Saxony, Brandenburg, Hesse (all Protestant); and Bavaria, Baden and Württemberg (all

Catholic). The Holy Roman Emperor Charles V, a Catholic, was forced to make a truce. It was known as the Peace of Augsburg (1555) and allowed the practice of "Lutheranism"—but not any other Protestant religion. Peace did not last. By 1618, the two groups were fighting the Thirty Years' War. Before long, other European nations became involved. When the treaty, the Peace of Westphalia, ended the war in 1648, much of the German farmland and cities had been destroyed.

Prussia Takes the Lead   In the late 1600's, Frederick-William, a member of the Hohenzollern family, ruled various German states, including Prussia. His son, Frederick I, and grandson, Frederick II (Frederick the Great), trained a strong army and civil service that unified their lands. They fought successfully in the War of the Austrian Succession and the Seven Years' War. Prussia became a dominant power in Europe.

In the late 1700's, the Prussians joined the Austrians to defend their lands against Napoleon when the French leader's armies invaded. But the Prussians had to give up territory east of the Elbe River. During Napoleon's invasion, the German people began to demand a new government that was more democratic, like governments recently formed in other parts of Europe, especially France.

The Congress of Vienna was held in 1815. Many of the German states, including Prussia, became united under Austrian rule. The congress established an assembly, the *Bundestag*, to represent each state. But this assembly could not solve the region's problems. Revolts occurred in Germany and Austria in 1848, but they were crushed.

Bismarck Builds a New Nation Otto von Bismarck became King William I's prime minister in 1862. Bismarck created the economic, social,

▲ *A German unification flag from 1832. Germany has been unified only rarely during its history.*

▲ *Otto von Bismarck, the "iron chancellor," who was responsible for the creation of a united Germany.*

GERMAN HISTORY TIMETABLE

about 500 B.C. The region now called Germany is invaded by Germanic tribes

about A.D. 500 Gaul (the regions we now call France and Germany) comes under the control of the Franks

751 Pepin the Short becomes King of the Franks, so founding the Carolingian dynasty (named for his son, Charlemagne)

843 The Frankish kingdom is divided, its eastern part becoming Germany

962 Otto I of Germany is crowned Holy Roman Emperor, and from now until the Empire's abolition in 1806 the German kings claim the title by right

1517 Martin Luther nails his "95 theses" to the church door in Wittenberg, and starts the Reformation

1618–1648 Germany is ravaged by the Thirty Years' War

1740 Frederick II, the Great, becomes King of Prussia, which he makes into a major European power

1806 Napoleon abolishes the Holy Roman Empire

1871 Prussia is victorious in the Franco-Prussian War, and the Prussian King William is crowned *Kaiser* (emperor) of a united Germany

1914 Germany's claim to new territories spark off World War I

1919 Germany, defeated in the war, becomes a republic

1934 Adolf Hitler adopts supreme power and takes the title *Führer* (leader)

1939 Hitler's invasion of Poland starts World War II

1945 Germany is defeated in the war, and is divided into four parts by the victorious Allies

1948 The Soviet Union cuts off all land links from the West to Berlin, but the other Allies fly in supplies (the Berlin Airlift) until, in 1949, the Soviets reopen the links

1954 The Communist eastern part of Germany achieves independence as the German Democratic Republic

1955 The three western parts of Germany together achieve independence as the Federal Republic of Germany

1961 The Soviet Union builds the Berlin Wall in an attempt to stop refugees escaping from East Germany to the West

◀ *A bronze statue of Charlemagne on his horse, made in the 800's.*

◀ *A German peasant revolt standard (banner) of the 1520's.*

▼ *The Prussian General Gebhard von Blucher, Wellington's ally at the Battle of Waterloo.*

▼ *Frederick the Great, the "Soldier King" of Prussia.*

► The famous Brandenburg Gate in Germany's premier city, Berlin.

► A German Messerschmidt fighter plane of World War II.

► Cover of a German satirical magazine in 1935. The Angel of Peace is suggesting to the Nobel Committee that they give the Peace Prize to Hitler.

▼ The Harvest of Battle, *a painting by C.R.W. Nevinson, shows wounded soldiers of World War I.*

▲ *In the 1920's Germany had such terrible inflation that money became worthless. Here, well-to-do Germans try to barter their silverware with a miller for sacks of flour.*

▼ *German dictator Adolf Hitler (right) and British prime minister Neville Chamberlain met at Munich in 1938. Chamberlain believed that Hitler had given him a guarantee of peace. A year later he was proved wrong.*

military, and political foundations that brought about German unity and supremacy. He introduced modern industrial techniques that rapidly expanded manufacturing activity, especially in such basic industries as steel, shipbuilding, and railroad equipment. Bismarck advised William to unify the Germans by adopting a policy of aggression toward other countries. He felt that a policy of "blood and iron" (military success and industrial progress) would guarantee national greatness. The Prussians successfully fought the Danes in 1864 and the Austrians two years later. From 1870 to 1871, Prussia fought with France in the Franco-Prussian War. The Prussians were again victorious.

Bismarck made a new constitution and a legislature. Citizens were able to vote for their representatives to the *Reichstag*, one of the houses in the legislature. Members of the other House, the *Bundesrat*, were appointed. The Prussian king, William, was crowned *Kaiser* (emperor) of all Germany in 1871. Meanwhile, other European nations that were already strongly united had taken over territory in other parts of the world.

William's grandson, William II, wanted his country to be as great as the others. He thought Bismarck's ways of doing things were too slow, so he dismissed him. The Kaiser claimed land in Africa. In Germany, new industries, transportation systems, and communication networks were expanded rapidly. The Germans also built a large fleet of ships. Other European nations became alarmed by Germany's growth. They made mutual defense treaties with one another for protection.

Germany in the 20th Century At the beginning of the 20th century there were many disputes over territory among European nations. One conflict was between Russia and Austria-Hungary over their interests in

the Balkans. Germany was a strong ally of Austria. On June 28, 1914, the Archduke Franz Ferdinand, heir to the Austro-Hungarian throne, was assassinated. All involved countries began to mobilize their armies. The Germans and the Austrians began to fight the British, French, and Russians. Other nations became involved in what was called the Great War (World War I). When the fighting ended four years later, the Germans and their allies were defeated. The Treaty of Versailles officially ended the war. Germany lost the territory it had seized from France during the Franco-Prussian War and all of its African colonies. The borders of Germany were redrawn, leaving many German-speaking people outside of the country. The Germans were ordered to pay about 33 billion dollars to the victors (which was never fully paid) and to give up their weapons.

Germany became a republic in 1919. The first national assembly met at Weimar, Germany, and the new German Reich was commonly referred to as the Weimar Republic. Many Germans were bitter about the harsh conditions of the Versailles Treaty. Many of them were unemployed and hungry. Miserable conditions made it possible for Adolf Hitler to become the nation's dictator in 1934. He was a member of the National Socialist, or *Nazi*, party that promised to return prosperity to the country. The Nazis ran a police state, with the Gestapo, or secret police, to punish or kill anyone whom they thought might be disloyal. Hitler took away the rights of Jewish citizens. During the next ten years, about six million Jews were killed by the Nazis in Germany and German-occupied countries.

Hitler called his state the Third Reich. He wanted his country to be the most important in the world. He thought that all German-speaking people should be under German rule—especially those in the areas

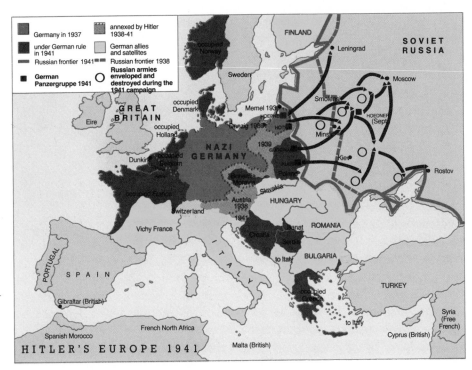

Germany in 1937 · **annexed by Hitler 1938-41** · **under German rule in 1941** · **German allies and satellites** · **Russian frontier 1941** · **Russian frontier 1938** · **German Panzergruppe 1941** · **Russian armies enveloped and destroyed during the 1941 campaign**

HITLER'S EUROPE 1941

◀ *This map shows the areas under control of Nazi Germany in 1941. At the end of that year, the United States entered the war.*

around Germany that were lost after World War I. The German people would have room to expand (*Lebensraum*). Hitler began to seize land bordering Germany in 1936. The other European nations failed to stop him. Hitler also rearmed his nation, violating the Versailles Treaty. Germany's neighbors also began to build up their armies. After Germany's invasion of Poland in 1939, other nations declared war and World War II began. Germany's army quickly overran much of Europe. But the course of the war changed in a few years, especially after the entry of the United States. The Germans and their allies were defeated in 1945.

After the war, Germany was again divided—into four parts. France, Russia, Great Britain, and the United States each controlled parts of Germany. East Germany, the Russian section, became a Communist nation called the German Democratic Republic. It is closely allied with the Soviet Union. The three other sections, West Germany, became the Federal Republic of Germany. Konrad Adenauer was its first chancellor.

The city of Berlin, which is entirely in East Germany, is divided by the Berlin Wall. The Communists built the wall in 1961 in an attempt to stop the flow of refugees out of East Berlin and East Germany. East Berlin is the capital of East Germany. West Berlin is a part of West Germany. Despite the wall, many people attempt to *defect* (cross over) from East to West. Some are shot by the Communist border guards, but most are successful. Some, in fact, *are* Communist border guards.

East and West Germany have ratified treaties calling for closer cultural and economic ties between them. However, many people living in these two countries today doubt that the two Germanies will ever again be united into one nation.

For further information on:
Events, *see* PROTESTANT REFORMATION, WORLD WAR I, WORLD WAR II.
Important People, *see* ADENAUER, KONRAD; BISMARCK, OTTO VON; HITLER, ADOLF; NAPOLEON BONAPARTE.
Institutions, *see* FASCISM, HOLY ROMAN EMPIRE.
Rulers, *see* CHARLES, HOLY ROMAN EMPERORS; FREDERICK, KINGS OF PRUSSIA; WILLIAM, KINGS OF GERMANY.

In 1948, the Soviet Union blockaded all routes joining Berlin with the rest of Western Germany. They hoped the blockade would force the Allies out of Berlin and that the people of West Berlin would be starved into accepting Communism. But the Allies began a huge airlift, and flew 8,000 tons of food and other supplies into Berlin every day. They kept this up for a year, and the Russians had to end their blockade.

Adolf Hitler set up the Hitler Youth organization. All German boys and girls had to join it. They learned Nazi beliefs, marched, and exercised. The Nazis taught the children to spy on everyone, even their own parents.

GERMAN LANGUAGE

German is the official language of the Federal Republic of Germany, the German Democratic Republic, Austria, and parts of Switzerland. It is related to other languages, including English, Dutch, Norwegian, Swedish, Danish, Flemish, and Icelandic.

Different varieties, or *dialects*, of German were spoken at one time. "High" German was used in the southern mountains and central highlands. But "Low" German was spoken in the northern plains. Martin Luther, religious leader, translated the Bible into High German during the 1500's. Luther's Bible helped make High German the language most Germans speak today.

For an idea of what German is like, a boy might introduce himself at school by saying "*Guten Morgen. Ich heisse Konrad.*" (Good morning. My name is Konrad.)

All nouns are capitalized in German. Although, with a few rare exceptions, the gender of English nouns is determined by sex—masculine for men, feminine for women, neuter for neither (objects)—there is not, necessarily, any relationship in German between the gender of the word and that of the object it symbolizes. For example, *Tür* (door) is feminine but *Mädchen* (girl) is neuter. The order of words in a sentence is often different in German from the normal order in English. Here is an English sentence with German word order. "My friends were worried, when I not at 10 o'clock on the bus arrived."

English developed from an ancient Low German dialect spoken by the Anglo-Saxons who settled England. Many German words are much like English. Can you guess the meanings of *Onkel*, *Wasser*, and *Haus*?

ALSO READ: ENGLISH LANGUAGE.

The "Iron Curtain," which separates East and West Germany, is 858 miles (1,380 km) long. It is a narrow strip of land 800 feet (240 m) wide, in which the East Germans have placed over two million land mines and 50,000 miles (80,000 km) of barbed wire.

GERMANY

Germany was once a single, large nation. Now the country is split into East Germany (Communist) and West Germany (a democracy). West Germany is twice as big as East Germany and has more than three times as many people.

A low, flat plain stretches across the north of both Germanies. Large river ports and many factories are in this region. Most of East Germany lies in the plain. The beautiful central highlands lie south of the plain. The Rhine and other rivers have cut gorges and valleys into the hills. On the rock banks of the Rhine are many castles. West Germany's capital, Bonn, is also on the Rhine.

Southern Germany is made up of rocky ridges. Rich farmlands are found in the lowlands between the ridges. A dark, thick forest of fir and spruce trees is in the southwest. This is the Black Forest, the scene of many German folk tales. Many tourists visit the healthful spas of the Black Forest

EAST GERMANY

Capital City: East Berlin (1,186,000 people).
Area: 41,768 square miles (108,178 sq. km).
Population: 16,700,000.
Government: Communist republic.
Natural Resources: Lignite, potash, uranium.
Export Products: Machinery, chemicals, precision instruments.
Unit of Money: Mark of the Deutsche Demokratische Republik.
Official Language: German.

WEST GERMANY

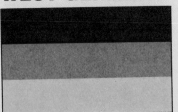

Capital City: Bonn (292,000 people).
Area: 95,976 square miles (248,577 sq. km).
Population: 61,000,000.
Government: Republic.
Natural Resources: Coal, iron ore, lumber, potash, some oil.
Export Products: Machinery and machine tools, chemicals, vehicles, iron and steel products, processed food.
Unit of Money: Deutsche Mark.
Official Language: German.

region. Resorts in the snow-capped Bavarian Alps of southern Germany are also famous.

Germany was divided after World War II. The victorious Allies split Germany into four zones. The war left most German cities in ruins. People were starving because farms could not produce enough food. West Germany recovered very rapidly from the war. It is now one of the world's leading industrial nations. In return, West Germany buys raw materials and food from other countries. East Germany had few industries before the war and it developed more slowly after 1945. Millions of people fled to West Germany when East Germany became a Communist country, creating a shortage of labor. But, with Soviet help, East Germany has become one of the world's top ten industrial powers and Europe's wealthiest Communist nation.

ALSO READ: BERLIN, COMMON MARKET, EUROPE, GERMAN HISTORY, GERMAN LANGUAGE, RHINE RIVER.

▼ *The Rhine is Europe's major river. There are countless fairy-tale castles along its banks in West Germany.*

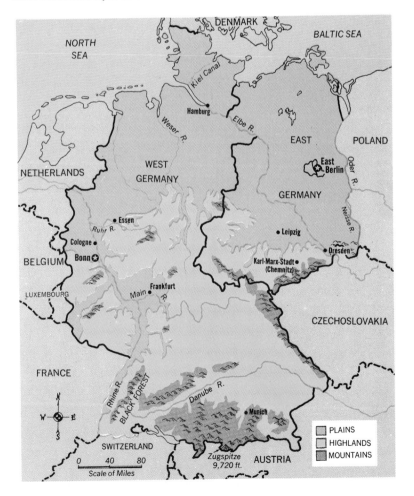

▲ *Geronimo, fierce rebel leader of the Chiricahua Apaches. He was also a man of few words. On his surrender in 1886 to Lieutenant-Colonel George Crook, he said: "Once I moved about like the wind. Now I surrender to you and that is all."*

▲ *The Gershwin brothers. George (top) was a great composer. Ira was a notable lyricist.*

GERMINATION see SEED.

GERONIMO (1829–1909) Geronimo was a well-known Indian leader and fighter. His Indian name was Goyathlay, or "one who yawns." But Geronimo, as the Mexicans called him, was not a slow, sleepy man. He became the brave and daring leader as well as medicine man of the Chiricahua Apache Indians.

North American settlers treated the Indians of the West badly. They forced tribes to give up their homelands and live on reservations. Geronimo rebelled against this practice and led a group of Apaches off their reservation in 1881. These Indians attacked white settlements, killing, burning homes, then vanishing. To avoid his pursuers, Geronimo and his followers fled into the mountains of northern Mexico. He surrendered in 1883, but left the reservation again in 1885. Geronimo was finally captured by U.S. Army troops in 1886.

Geronimo was then sent as a prisoner of war to Florida and, later, to Alabama. He finally settled at Fort Sill, Oklahoma. He published his life story, called *Geronimo: His Own Story*, in 1906.

ALSO READ: APACHE INDIANS, INDIAN WARS.

GERSHWIN, GEORGE AND IRA Two talented brothers, George and Ira Gershwin, are among the most distinguished in the history of U.S. music. George Gershwin (1898–1937) wrote the first serious jazz music for orchestra to be played in a concert hall. Ira Gershwin (1896–1983) was a *lyricist*, a writer of words for songs. He worked with his composer brother on several musical comedy shows.

Both brothers were born in Brooklyn, New York. George had some musical training as a boy. He worked as a pianist for publishers of popular music. His song "Swanee" became a hit when singer Al Jolson recorded it in 1919. However, George wanted to write a more serious type of music based on jazz. His chance came when bandleader Paul Whiteman asked him to write a piece of music for a jazz concert in New York City. His famous work for piano and orchestra, *Rhapsody in Blue*, was the result. It was first performed on February 12, 1924, with George playing the solo piano part. Other orchestral works, such as *An American in Paris*, followed.

Ira Gershwin began to work with George in 1924. Together, they wrote a number of popular musical comedies, including *Funny Face* and *Strike Up the Band*. In 1931, *Of Thee I Sing* became the first musical comedy to win the Pulitzer Prize.

The Gershwin brothers' greatest work was the American folk opera *Porgy and Bess*, which was about black life in a Southern city. Not long after it was first produced, George died of a brain tumor. Ira Gershwin continued to write lyrics and received many honors.

ALSO READ: JAZZ, MUSIC, MUSICAL COMEDY.

GESTATION see REPRODUCTION.

GETTYSBURG ADDRESS A long, bloody battle fought at Gettysburg, Pennsylvania, from July 1 to July 3, 1863, became the turning point of the American Civil War. Nearly 5,000 Union and Confederate soldiers were killed, and more than 38,000 men were wounded. But the Union Army managed to turn back the Confederates' last major invasion of the North. Both sides paid a great price, and the entire nation, both North and South, was stunned and saddened.

The battlefield at Gettysburg was dedicated as a soldiers' cemetery on November 19, 1863. Today this cemetery is a national monument where more than 45,000 Civil War dead are buried. Many famous people came to Gettysburg to give speeches at the dedication ceremonies. President Abraham Lincoln was one of them.

President Lincoln had been so busy directing the war that he had little time to prepare his speech. He wrote it while traveling on a train to Gettysburg, and he made several changes as he read his speech to the crowd. The people had just listened to a two-hour speech given by a famous orator (speechmaker) of that time, Edward Everett. Everett's speech was considered to be very impressive by all the newspapers, while Lincoln's speech was practically ignored. Everett himself was one of the few to be aware of the greatness of Lincoln's words.

The contrast between what Everett said in two hours and what Lincoln said in two minutes only serves to highlight the greatness of Lincoln's words. The speech was sincere and brief, and it managed to express all the ideals of the people of the United States. Today the Gettysburg Address is considered to be not only a classic example of a good speech (short and "to-the-point"), but also one of the most moving expressions of democratic principles and spirit ever spoken.

GETTYSBURG ADDRESS

"Four score and seven years ago our fathers brought forth on this continent, a new nation, conceived in Liberty, and dedicated to the proposition that all men are created equal.

Now we are engaged in a great civil war, testing whether that nation, or any nation so conceived and so dedicated, can long endure. We are met on a great battlefield of that war. We have come to dedicate a portion of that field, as a final resting place for those who here gave their lives that that nation might live. It is altogether fitting and proper that we should do this.

But, in a larger sense, we can not dedicate—we can not consecrate—we can not hallow—this ground. The brave men, living and dead, who struggled here, have consecrated it, far above our poor power to add or detract. The world will little note, nor long remember what we say here, but it can never forget what they did here. It is for us the living, rather, to be dedicated here to the unfinished work which they who fought here have thus far so nobly advanced. It is rather for us to be here dedicated to the great task remaining before us—that from these honored dead we take increased devotion to that cause for which they gave the last full measure of devotion—that we here highly resolve that these dead shall not have died in vain—that this nation, under God, shall have a new birth of freedom—and that government of the people, by the people, for the people, shall not perish from the earth."

ALSO READ: AMERICAN HISTORY; CIVIL WAR; LINCOLN, ABRAHAM.

GEYSER Have you ever watched a teakettle when the water boils? Steam comes out of the spout in a steady stream. A geyser also is produced by boiling water and escaping steam.

In a few places in the surface of the Earth there are tubelike cracks that reach down to the hot rock inside. Rainwater and water from underground springs collect in these cracks. If the crack is crooked, the hot water is trapped and gets hotter and hotter.

The weight of the water in the tube increases the pressure at the bottom. The increased pressure makes it possible for the water to be heated above its normal boiling temperature of 212° F (100° C) without boiling. But the water keeps getting hotter until it does boil. This pushes water out of the top of the tube. The loss of this water lessens the pressure on the water at the bottom. Because this water is already far above its normal boiling point, the lessened pressure causes it to boil suddenly, turning to steam. A column of water and steam gushes out as a geyser whenever the water at the bottom becomes hot enough to boil.

Geysers are very rare. They exist mainly in Iceland, New Zealand, and in the western United States. Most

Lincoln wrote five drafts of the Gettysburg Address. Two copies are in the Library of Congress. The last draft, written in 1864, was later engraved inside the Lincoln Memorial in Washington, D.C.

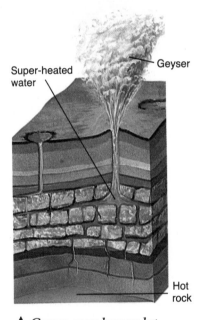

▲ *Geysers occur because hot rocks underground heat water under pressure. Because of the pressure, the water is heated to temperatures far above water's normal boiling point. When a little water leaks out at the top of the geyser, the pressure on the rest is decreased. Abruptly all the rest boils, and a powerful jet of water and steam is pushed out of the ground.*

GHANA

The biggest geyser in the world is Waimangu in New Zealand. It erupted to a height of more than 1,500 feet (457 m) in 1904. It has not been active since 1917.

erupt at unpredictable intervals. Old Faithful, at Yellowstone National Park, is quite regular, and averages one spectacular eruption every 66½ minutes.

ALSO READ: EARTH, TEMPERATURE SCALE, VOLCANO.

GHANA The West African republic of Ghana includes the former British colony known as the Gold Coast and the former U.N. Trust Territory of Togoland. The country became independent in 1957. Its name is the same as a kingdom that existed in present-day Mali between the 700's and 1100's.

Ghana's neighbors are the Ivory Coast on the west, Togo on the east, and Burkina Faso on the north. The Gulf of Guinea, an arm of the Atlantic Ocean, forms the southern boundary. Ghana is a little more than twice the size of Pennsylvania. (See the map with the article on AFRICA.)

Much of the country has temperatures above 80° F (27° C) and receives 40 to 60 inches (100 to 150 cm) of rainfall annually. Forests cover large areas in the southwest, but the drier north has treeless, grassy plains called *savannas*. Along the coast is a flat, sandy plain. Hills and plateaus lie inland. The Volta River winds the length of the country.

More than half of the people of Ghana are farmers. They raise much of the food the country needs. They

▲ Accra, the capital of Ghana. The city was founded in the 1600's around European trading posts.

often keep chickens, sheep, and goats. They grow several crops for export, especially cacao, of which Ghana is the world's leading exporter. Other agricultural products are coffee, kola nuts, coconuts, rubber, and palm oil and palm seeds. Ghana has rich deposits of gold, diamonds, manganese, and bauxite. Since the completion of the Akosombo Dam on the Volta River in 1966, the country has had electric power for industrial development. Electricity is used to run an aluminum smelter at Tema.

English is the official language of Ghana. The people speak approximately 100 languages and dialects and often cannot understand each other unless they speak English. Today about two-fifths of the people live in

GHANA

Capital City: Accra (860,000 people).
Area: 92,100 square miles (238,537 sq. km).
Population: 14,300,000.
Government: The Provisional National Defense Council rules the country.
Natural Resources: Bauxite, diamonds, gold, manganese.
Export Products: Cacao, lumber, gold.
Unit of Money: Cedi.
Official Language: English.

cities. Accra is the capital, largest city, and major seaport.

Ghana's first president, Kwame Nkrumah, ruled like a dictator from 1960 until army officers overthrew him in 1966. Since then, Ghana has been governed mainly by various military groups, although there have been some short periods of civilian rule.

ALSO READ: AFRICA.

GHOST A pale, wavering, shifting form seemingly made of fog appears. Is it a ghost? Or is it only a curtain moving in the breeze? The word "ghost" (or "apparition") means the spirit of a person who has died.

People believed in ancient times that, when people died, their spirits or ghosts stayed on Earth. People offered gifts of food and clothing to make a ghost go away or to make its life after death more pleasant.

The traditional kind of ghost is usually said to be seen lurking in graveyards, or wandering about old houses and castles. Ghosts are normally seen only at night. They sometimes warn people of danger. In other cases, they are said to return to Earth because of something that happened in their previous lives. Persons may have committed crimes or died with guilty secrets. They may have had an unnatural death or an improper burial. Their ghosts may return to *haunt* (continually visit) the places where they lived or the people who wronged them in life. Buildings that supposedly have ghosts are said to be "haunted."

Ghosts have been the subject of countless stories, plays, poems, and even operas. William Shakespeare wrote several plays in which ghosts appear. One such play is *Hamlet*. In Charles Dickens's story *A Christmas Carol*, Scrooge is frightened by Marley's ghost, whose rattling chains and moaning he hears. Ghosts also play an important part in many religions.

A British organization, the Society for Psychical Research, was formed in 1882 to look into many reports of ghost-sightings. A similar organization exists in the United States. No proof has been found that ghosts are real, but investigators continue to study the causes of unexplained incidents. Several journals deal with psychic phenomena.

GIANT The myths of many countries tell of giants. People made up giants to represent—or to explain—forces in nature, such as earthquakes, floods, and the movement of the planets, that confused them.

In Greek mythology, Atlas was a giant who held the heavens on his shoulders. Greek and Roman myths describe an entire race of giants, called Titans, who lived on the Earth before people did. Prometheus was a Titan who was believed to have taught people the secret of fire. People explained the violent earthquakes and volcanic eruptions of the time by saying that the Titans were fighting the gods for control of the world. As centuries passed and there seemed to be fewer earthquakes and volcanoes, people added to their myths the defeat of the Titans by the superior power of the gods.

Scandinavian myths also tell about many giants who were almost the equals of their gods in strength and daring. Many giants were friendly to people, but Scandinavians believed that landslides and sudden floods were caused by angry giants.

Goliath, in an Old Testament story, was a Philistine giant. The Philistines tried to invade the land belonging to the Hebrews. During a battle, the human-sized David, armed only with a slingshot, managed to kill Goliath and defeat the Philistines.

Giants are a popular subject in literature. Homer, a famous Greek

▲ *Most Ghanaians live in villages such as this one located along Ghana's sandy coastal plain.*

▼ *Some startling photographs exist of what appear to be ghosts. This is supposed to show the "Brown Lady" descending the stairs at Raynham Hall, Norfolk, England. Several famous people have said that they have seen her. She is thought to be Dorothy, the sister of British politician Sir Robert Walpole (1676–1745).*

▲ *Dutch giant Jan van Albert towers over his midget friend.*

poet, wrote about a race of one-eyed giants, called Cyclopes, in his epic poem *The Odyssey*. The Cyclopes, descendants of the Titans, were shepherds who lived on an island.

The French writer François Rabelais wrote in the 1500's about a giant named Gargantua and his son, Pantagruel, who were famous for their huge appetites. Rabelais used these giants both to satirize (make fun of) customs of the time and to recommend changes in human beings and society.

Gulliver's Travels (1726), written by Jonathan Swift, contains another famous story about giants. Gulliver traveled to a land of giants called Brobdingnags. Swift also used his giants to satirize customs of the time. But the story is very entertaining even when the satire is not considered.

Probably the most famous U.S. giant is the legendary Paul Bunyan. His feet were said to be so large that when his footprints filled with rainwater they became the Great Lakes!

Giants in Fact Many of the legends about giants may have had some basis in fact. There *are* people who are so abnormally large that doctors consider them giants. Although giants in stories are unusually strong, *real* giants are physically much weaker than ordinary people.

When the pituitary gland, which controls growth, produces too much of its hormone, it causes the condition called *giantism* or *gigantism*. But a giant's size does not give him greater strength. The muscles and organs of the human body are not strong enough to control such a large skeleton. Giantism can occasionally be controlled with surgery or X rays. But, because of the immense strain on their bodies from supporting their size, giants usually die young.

ALSO READ: BUNYAN, PAUL; GLAND; HORMONE; MYTHOLOGY; SWIFT, JONATHAN; TITAN.

GIBRALTAR In the narrow waterway that connects the Atlantic Ocean with the Mediterranean Sea stands the majestic Rock of Gibraltar. On its southern side, the Strait of Gibraltar separates the Rock from North Africa. A narrow, sandy strip of land on its northwestern side links it to Spain. The Rock and this strip of land make up the tiny British crown colony of Gibraltar.

The colony covers only 2½ square miles (6.5 sq. km). The limestone Rock rises about 1,400 feet (427 m) above the water. It is full of natural caves and fortified tunnels. In Gibraltar live large, tailless monkeys called Barbary apes, the only wild monkeys in Europe.

The town of Gibraltar is on the west side of the Rock. The houses in the town are set close together on narrow streets. Gibraltar has no natural resources. But it has been an important naval and military base because it controls the passage between the Atlantic Ocean and the Mediterranean Sea. Arabs (and later the Spanish) have controlled Gibraltar. The British captured it in 1704 and have turned Gibraltar into a modern fortress. Spain claims Gibraltar. But in 1967 the 30,000 people of Gibraltar (who are mostly of Spanish, Italian, and Maltese descent) voted to stay under British rule.

ALSO READ: MEDITERRANEAN SEA.

GIBSON, ALTHEA (born 1927) The rise of a young black girl from New York City to U.S. and British tennis championships is one of the most remarkable success stories in the world of sports.

Althea Gibson was born in Silver, South Carolina, and grew up in New York City. She learned to play tennis on streets that were blocked to traffic and used as playgrounds. In 1950, Althea Gibson was the first black per-

▼ *The Rock of Gibraltar has stood for ages as a symbol of strength.*

son to play in an important national tennis tournament. In 1951, she was the first member of her race to participate in the tennis matches at Wimbledon, in London, England.

Each year, the best tennis players in the world play in the Wimbledon tournament. It was there, in 1957 and in 1958, that Althea Gibson won the women's singles championship. She then teamed up with three other women tennis players and won the doubles championship for three years in a row.

In the United States, Miss Gibson won the national women's singles title in 1957 and 1958. She also won the mixed-doubles championship with Kurt Nielson in 1957.

Althea Gibson retired from tennis in 1958. A superb athlete, she then became a professional golfer.

GILBERT, SIR HUMPHREY
see NEWFOUNDLAND-LABRADOR.

GILBERT AND SULLIVAN
Two Englishmen, William Gilbert and Arthur Sullivan, worked together between 1871 and 1896, writing comic operas, or *operettas*. Their works have delighted audiences ever since. Their best-known works are probably *The Mikado*, *The Pirates of Penzance*, and *H.M.S. Pinafore*.

These operettas have light and amusing stories, or plots. The spoken words and the lyrics of the songs often poke fun at life in Britain under the reign of Queen Victoria.

Both men produced many works separately, but they are chiefly remembered for the 14 "Gilbert and Sullivan" operettas, in which Gilbert wrote the *librettos*, or words, and Sullivan wrote the music. The two men were brought together by a music *impresario*, or manager, Richard D'Oyly Carte (1844–1901). He became their business manager and formed the D'Oyly Carte Opera

Company to produce their works. He even built a theater, the Savoy, in London for them. Their works are sometimes called the "Savoy Operas." Fans of Gilbert and Sullivan and touring theater companies that perform their operettas are often called "Savoyards."

William Schwenck Gilbert (1836–1911) was born in London. After attending college, he began writing poems called the *Bab Ballads*, which made fun of some of the people and the customs of his time. He wrote a number of plays in addition to the librettos for the Gilbert and Sullivan operettas. In his librettos, Gilbert created fantastically absurd characters and situations. His *parodies* (ridiculous exaggerations) often offended Queen Victoria, but he was knighted by King Edward VII in 1907.

Arthur Seymour Sullivan (1842–1900) was also born in London. He began to compose music at an early age. Sullivan produced many fine hymn tunes, including the famous "Onward, Christian Soldiers." He also wrote long choral pieces, known as *oratorios*. Sullivan always felt that his best work was the religious popular song "The Lost Chord." He was knighted by Queen Victoria in 1883.

ALSO READ: OPERA.

GIOTTO DI BONDONE (about 1267–1337)
Giotto was born near Florence, Italy, the son of a poor farmer. According to legend, the young Giotto was tending a flock of sheep one day. To pass the time, he began to sketch one of the sheep with a rough, pointed stone on a smooth surface of rock. As he was drawing, a famous artist, Giovanni Cimabue, happened to come by. The artist was so impressed by the boy's talent that he invited Giotto to come to Florence and be his pupil.

Before Giotto, European artists painted in a flat, *linear* style that had

▲ *Althea Gibson playing for the women's tennis championship at Wimbledon, England.*

▼ *Gilbert and Sullivan are famous for their operettas. William Gilbert (top) wrote the words. Arthur Sullivan (bottom) wrote the music.*

▲ The Flight into Egypt, *by the Italian painter Giotto.*

Giotto painted frescoes that have lasted. Frescoes are difficult to make. The artist must paint on wet plaster, working very fast and doing only a section at a time. The plaster and paints must be mixed exactly the same for each section, otherwise the colors will not match.

not changed in 500 years. Their style is called linear because it depended on the use of lines rather than shapes. Giotto discovered how to make a flat surface look as if it has depth. He gave his figures a three-dimensional look—height, width, and depth—so that they seem almost as solid-looking as sculpture.

Look at Giotto's painting, *The Flight into Egypt.* Your eye goes directly to Mary holding the baby Jesus. The donkey seems to be stepping carefully, aware of the precious burden he is carrying. Joseph looks back to see that they are all coming along safely. Notice that this entire scene takes place in the *foreground* (toward the front) of the painting. Also, most of the activity takes place in the bottom half of the picture. In these ways, Giotto makes the viewer almost enter into the picture. He was the first painter to try to make the

viewers feel as if they were part of the painting.

The Flight into Egypt is a *fresco* (a painting done on damp plaster). It is one of the 38 Scrovegni frescoes he painted from 1305 to 1310 in the Arena Chapel in the city of Padua, Italy. The little chapel had just been built. It was a simple building, 134 feet (41 m) long, with only six windows on one side. On its smooth walls, Giotto painted the early life of the Virgin Mary and the life of Christ. These frescoes are among the greatest Italian works of art.

Almost nothing is known of Giotto's life before his marvelous frescoes made him famous. Later he decorated two other chapels and became a leading painter and architect in Florence. Giotto's way of painting was further developed by others during the Renaissance.

ALSO READ: ART HISTORY, PAINTING, RENAISSANCE.

GIRAFFE The giraffe is the tallest animal on the Earth. Because it is so tall, a giraffe can eat the leaves in a treetop. Long legs and a neck over six feet (1.8 m) long give the animal its height. Males average over 18 feet (5.5 m) from the ground to their ears.

A giraffe's face is gentle, with big brown eyes whose thick lashes keep dust out. It can also completely cover its nostrils to protect its nose. It lives in the open country of Africa, where there is often dust and no water, and can go for a long time without water, like a camel. It gets some water from leaves, stripping them off limbs with its tongue. A giraffe chews its cud, like cattle, goats, and deer. Giraffes have short, covered horns.

Because of its long neck, the giraffe must spread its legs far apart in order to lower its head to drink water. Its enemy, the African lion, senses this weakness and often attacks a drinking giraffe. But the giraffe has good sight, hearing, and smell to warn it of danger. If it is frightened, it gallops at about 30 miles (48 km) an hour. Its color also helps hide it—brown blotches on a tan coat look like leaves in the sun. If a giraffe is cornered, it kicks with both front and hind legs.

Giraffes are sociable animals. They live in small groups led by a mature male, and feed with ostriches and other animals. Birds called oxpeckers ride on their backs and eat fleas. Their frightened flight warns giraffes of danger.

A baby giraffe is six feet (1.8 m) tall when born. It can stand alone in a few minutes, and runs well in two days.

ALSO READ: MAMMAL.

GIRL SCOUTS see YOUNG PEOPLE'S ASSOCIATIONS.

GLACIER What do you think would happen to snow if it did not melt? In most parts of the world, days become warmer in spring and the snow melts. But in a few regions, more snow falls during the year than can melt away. Glaciers, huge masses of snow and ice that can slide over the ground, form from the snow. How does this happen?

As snow piles high, it has great weight. As one snowfall piles on top of another, the weight changes the snow on the bottom of the pile into ice. The ice becomes thicker and thicker, and then begins very slowly to move. The thickness needed to start movement depends upon how steep the mountain is. Have you ever been sledding on a hill? Your sled starts moving sooner and moves faster on a steep hill than on a gentle slope. The speed at which a glacier advances also depends upon how large it is. Glaciers in the Alps move an average of a foot (30 cm) a day. In Greenland, glaciers move about 60 feet (18 m) a day.

Glaciers today form only in the Arctic, the Antarctic, and on very high mountains. During ice ages, of which there have been at least five, glaciers frequently cover wide areas of the Earth.

Scientists describe several kinds of

▲ *The giraffe is the tallest animal in the world.*

▼ *Glaciers are found in cold places, either near the North and South poles, or high in the mountains. Mountain glaciers flow like rivers, but much more slowly.*

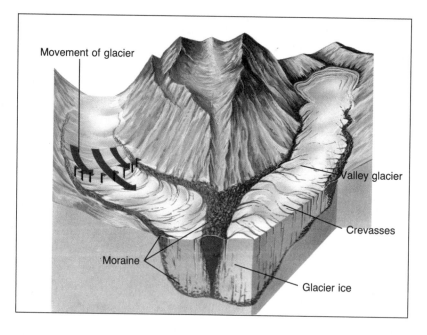

Movement of glacier

Valley glacier

Crevasses

Moraine

Glacier ice

▲ *Glaciers move under their own weight. As more and more snow is added to the top of the glacier, the pressure on the ice nearest the ground increases. Because of the pressure, this ice melts slightly. The glacier inches forward on this melted layer. When glaciers melt, they leave behind them the debris that they carried with them. This* moraine *remains behind as mounds of rocky material.*

The ice in glaciers moves very slowly, usually only a few inches a year. However, sometimes things speed up. In 1936, the Black Rapids Glacier in Alaska advanced by more than 200 feet (60 m) a day.

glaciers. Two important kinds are *valley glaciers* and *ice sheets*. Valley glaciers flow down through the valleys of mountains such as the Alps or the Rockies. Rocks on the underside and sides of these glaciers scrape the valleys, making them wider and deeper. A valley enlarged by a glacier is U-shaped. A valley glacier melts when it reaches the warmer weather of the lowlands.

An *ice sheet* is a broad mass of ice that spreads outward in all directions. Greenland and Antarctica are covered by vast ice sheets. At the ocean edges the ice sheets *calve*—that is, pieces break off to become icebergs.

ALSO READ: ICE AGE, ICEBERG.

GLADIATOR The spectacle of men fighting in public contests, usually to the death, was a popular form of entertainment in ancient Rome. Gladiators were trained fighters who battled each other in huge public arenas. The crowd would cheer their favorites.

At first, gladiators were slaves, prisoners of war, and criminals who were forced to fight in contests. They were often kept in chains when they were not fighting. But Roman citizens

also trained to become gladiators in order to demonstrate their strength and skill. Gladiators sometimes won large sums of money and became famous.

Gladiatorial contests were usually man-to-man, but women, dwarfs, and wild animals were sometimes put into the arena. Gladiators fought to the death, but if one man were losing, the crowd could save him by waving their handkerchiefs. If they wanted him to die, they would turn down their thumbs.

Many successful gladiators became famous. Spartacus, a slave turned gladiator, once led an unsuccessful slave rebellion. In A.D. 325 the emperor Constantine tried to abolish the cruel and bloody gladiatorial contests, but, because of their popularity, they continued to be held for another 175 years.

ALSO READ: ROMAN EMPIRE, SPARTACUS.

GLAND Glands are organs found in the bodies of plants and animals. Glands *secrete* (produce and send out) various chemical substances. The glands in your body are so important that, if one of them is not working properly, it can cause serious illness or even death.

There are two main kinds of glands in your body. *Endocrine* glands secrete hormones directly into the bloodstream without passing them through a tube, or *duct*. For this reason, endocrine glands are often called *ductless* glands. *Exocrine* glands secrete substances onto the surfaces of body tissues through ducts.

The ductless glands are located in various parts of the body and do various jobs. The *pituitary* gland, located at the base of the brain, is the master ductless gland of the body. The pituitary gland helps control the growth of the whole body. It also produces hormones that control almost all of the other glands. The *parathyroid* glands, located in the neck, produce a hormone that is necessary for normal bone growth. The *adrenal* glands that lie on top of the kidneys secrete many hormones. One, adrenaline, controls the rate of your breathing and heartbeat when you are frightened or scared. The *thyroid* gland, located around the trachea (windpipe) in the neck, secretes two hormones that control the rate at which the body uses energy. The *sex* glands secrete hormones that have important effects on a person's appearance, emotions, and ability to have children. The *liver* secretes bile, which helps the body to digest fats. (The liver has many other important functions—it is the "chemical factory" of the body.) The pancreas, an exocrine gland located near the liver, contains little masses of cells called the *Islets of Langerhans*, which are ductless glands. They produce insulin and glucagon, two hormones that help to control the amount of sugar in your blood.

There are many kinds of exocrine glands. Some are just tubes, or ducts, of various shapes. Others are in two parts—one part forming the duct, the second part forming the organ that produces the secretions. The *pancreas* is an exocrine gland that secretes digestive juices into the duodenum (the part of the small intestine that attaches to the stomach). Sweat is given off by millions of *sweat* glands all over the skin. *Salivary* glands secrete saliva that helps break down food in the mouth and begin the process of digestion. There are glands in the breasts that produce milk for babies, and there are glands in the eyes that produce tears to keep your eyes clear of harmful substances.

Plants and animals have glands, too. The nectar of flowers is produced by glands. The silk that a spider uses to make its web comes from the spider's glands. The shells of oysters are built from gland secretions. In trees,

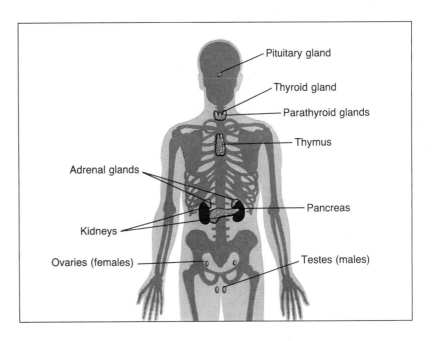

glands produce a sticky substance called resin.

ALSO READ: CIRCULATORY SYSTEM, DIGESTION, GIANT, HORMONE, LIVER, METABOLISM.

▲ *The major glands of the human body.*

GLASS   Look around you and see how many objects you can find that are made of glass. You will probably see windowpanes at first and then drinking glasses, bottles, and mirrors. Perhaps you are reading these words through "glasses," or optical lenses. Thousands of everyday objects are made of glass or contain some glass—from playing marbles to tires. Glass is one of the most useful materials in the world.

What is Glass?   Believe it or not, glass is actually a liquid! However, it has such high *viscosity* (it flows so slowly) that for all practical purposes it can be thought of as a solid.

Glass may vary from black *opaque* (unable to be seen through) substances, such as the mineral obsidian, to colorless, transparent manufactured glasses, such as optical lenses. The physical properties of glasses also vary according to their composition. The properties of glass can be con-

▼ *A glass vessel made in Syria during the time of the ancient Romans.*

GLASS

▲ *A glassblower blows a bubble of glass at the end of a pipe. When the bubble is the size wanted, he can shape the glass using iron rods, or spin it into a flat disk.*

In some ways glass is like a very thick liquid. Although it seems very hard, over hundreds of years it will flow into a different shape. If you should look closely at ancient window glass in a European church, you might find that the glass is thicker at the bottom than at the top. The glass has very slowly run downward.

trolled in manufacture, so it is possible to use the material for many purposes, from walls of buildings to jewelry.

The materials going into glass vary according to what it will be used for, but the chief raw material in manufacturing glass is sand. Various chemicals are added to the sand. The chemicals give the glass its particular properties or characteristics. Some chemicals help to purify the glass, preventing distortion. Seeing a clear image without distortion is extremely important in optical lenses. Other chemicals give the glass color or make it heat-resistant. For example, glass used in cookware or some thermometers has to be able to withstand extremely high temperatures.

Very often fragments of broken glass, called *cullet*, are added to the mixture. This is what is done with the soda bottles you return to the grocery store. In this way, glass is "recycled," and there is no unnecessary waste to pollute the environment.

The mixture of sand, cullet, and chemicals is heated in a furnace at such a high temperature that it melts. For the modern-day mass production of glass articles, "tank furnaces," which can hold 1,000 tons (900 metric tons) of glass at one time, are used. The raw materials are fed continuously into an opening in one end of the tank, while the *molten* (melted) glass is drawn off at the other end.

There are several methods of working glass while it is soft. Plate glass for windows is made by rolling a sheet of soft glass between large rollers. A more modern process is to float molten glass in a layer on top of a bath of molten metal. In this way a continuous sheet of glass is made. Other techniques work glass in a variety of ways.

Pressing and casting are the oldest forms of glass-working. Presses force the glass into casts, or molds. The outside surface of the object is formed by the mold itself. A plunger is forced

into the mold to shape the inside surface.

Glass can also be shaped with a blowpipe, an iron pipe, about four feet (1.2 m) long, with a mouthpiece at one end. The glassblower dips up a small amount of molten glass on the end of the pipe. The worker rolls or presses the gob of glass against a paddle or metal plate to shape its outside surface and then blows into the mouthpiece, producing a bubble of glass. By twisting the blowpipe while blowing, and by rolling and shaping with a paddle, a great variety of shapes can be made. When the object is completed but still soft, it is cut away from the pipe with scissors. Glassblowing is a delicate art, and glass that is blown by highly skilled craftworkers is both beautiful and valuable.

Most mass-produced glassware today is produced by glassblowing done by machines. Molten glass is poured continuously over a nozzle through which a blast of air is forced.

After they are formed, all glass objects are *annealed*. This means they are subjected to a high temperature and then slowly cooled. This process

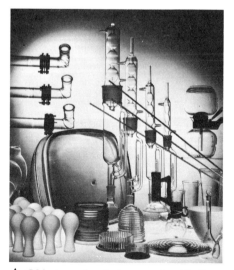

▲ *Objects made of glass are durable (but most will break if you drop them), usually unbendable, and often very beautiful. Glass products are common in the home and in industry. Can you identify any of these?*

balances the tensions on the inside and outside of the object, producing a glass of great toughness. At this stage, several other processes, chiefly for decoration, might be performed. These include polishing, engraving, cutting, and enameling.

The Countless Uses of Glass

Thousands of variations in the glassmaking process are used to produce glass for different purposes. Imagine what can be done with a material that can be seen through, can resist heat, acid, and rusting, and can be made stronger than steel!

SAFETY GLASS. The glass used in automobile windows and eyeglasses is called "safety glass." It is made by *lamination*, placing thin sheets of transparent plastic between two sheets of plate glass. When safety glass is broken, the pieces of glass stick to the layer of plastic instead of shattering.

FIBERGLASS. Molten glass that is forced through small holes in metal plates, producing extremely thin fibers, can be woven and bent as easily as wool or cotton. Glass fibers that have been woven into fabrics make excellent materials for drapery and upholstery because of their resistance to fire and water. Glass fabrics are also used for insulating storage batteries (they cannot be damaged by acid), and insulating the walls of buildings (they keep in heat and absorb noise).

GLASS AND PLASTIC. By combining fiberglass with plastics (*synthetic resins*), it is possible to produce solid molded objects that combine the strength of steel with the resistance of glass. Glass-and-plastic boat hulls are unaffected by salt water or barnacles. Strips of this material are added to the rubber in "belted" automobile tires, making them extremely strong.

GLASS IN SCIENCE. Glass containing a large amount of lead has been found to provide an excellent shield against radiation. Such glass is used for the protection of doctors and technicians

who work with X rays. It is also used to protect personnel working in nuclear-energy plants. Since all this glass is transparent, it not only provides protection from radiation, but also enables the worker to observe nuclear reactors in operation.

A Centuries-old Process Glass appeared on Earth in a "natural state" long before people learned how to make it themselves. Slender glass tubes, called *fulgurites*, are often found on beaches that have been struck by lightning. The heat of the lightning has fused the sand and any other matter near it into glass. Shiny black glass, called obsidian, is found around volcanoes all over the world. The sand and rocks have been heated in the "furnace" of the volcano. Primitive people have used obsidian for making knives, jewelry, and money.

No one is sure exactly when or where people began to make glass themselves. Scientists have found manmade glass relics in the Middle East that date from 3000 B.C. The manufacture of glass was widespread in the Middle East at least 500 years before the birth of Christ. But the process was slow and expensive. Only wealthy kings and priests could afford glass objects.

The invention of glassblowing by the Phoenicians about 100 B.C. revolutionized the manufacture of glass. Now glassworkers could shape glass into any creative or useful form that they wanted. Glass was no longer a luxury. Glassmaking became an im-

▲ *This beautiful crystal vase has* kinnaras, *mythical Thai creatures, etched into the glass.*

▼ *In a factory, molten glass can be shaped in a number of different ways. Bottles can be made using molds. Sheet glass can be produced either by using water-cooled rollers, or by allowing the molten glass to spread out over a "lake" of molten metal.*

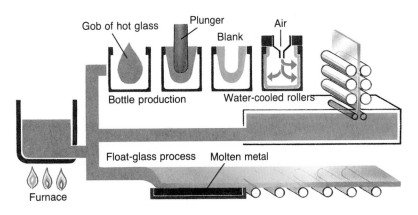

▲ *This woman is carrying enough glass-fiber cable to do the work of the great drum of ordinary copper cable behind her.*

▼ *Benjamin Franklin invented bifocal glasses. He could wear them for both reading and for general vision.*

portant industry in the ancient world. Windows, at first made from blown glass, appeared about A.D. 100.

When Roman conquerors returned to Europe from the Middle East, they brought the knowledge of glassmaking with them. But when the Roman Empire fell, glassmaking was forgotten in Europe for the next century. In the 1200's, craftworkers in Venice, Italy, rediscovered the method of creating glass articles. They turned glassmaking into an extremely beautiful art. Venetian glass, with its delicate patterns that resemble lace, is still valued and admired throughout the world.

By the late 1600's, glassmaking flourished throughout Europe. Colonists brought the art to North America. Today it is one of the United States's largest industries. With constant experimentation, hundreds of new forms of glass have been created, giving glass thousands of new uses. The most modern inventions, such as lasers and fiber optics, have created even more uses for this material. Who can tell what thousands of new uses will be found for glass in the future?

ALSO READ: AQUARIUM, BAROMETER, CLOCKS AND WATCHES, FIBER OPTICS, GLASSES, KALEIDOSCOPE, LASER AND MASER, LENS, MICROSCOPE, MIRROR, STAINED GLASS, SYNTHETIC, TELESCOPE.

GLASSES You could not read the words on this page if your eyes did not provide good vision. The letters would appear to be blurred or fuzzy. People who have imperfect eyesight can wear glasses in front of their eyes to improve their vision.

Glasses, sometimes called eyeglasses or spectacles, are made in a wide variety of shapes. The most common form of glasses consists of a pair of *lenses* (molded pieces of glass) in a metal or plastic frame that fits over the bridge of the nose. The glass

of the lenses is cut and shaped according to the needs of the wearer. The lenses will bend the light rays to the angle needed to correct the particular eye defect.

It is not known exactly when people first began using glasses to correct eye defects. A lens was found in the 3,500-year-old ruins of ancient Babylon. The Roman emperor Nero used a lenslike jewel mounted on his ring to watch gladiator fights. By late medieval times eyeglasses were common. In 1760 bifocals were made for Benjamin Franklin at his suggestion. In bifocal lenses the upper half of each lens is ground for distant vision and the lower half is ground for close vision. Glass contact lenses were invented in 1887. Since these lenses are worn directly on the eyeball, there is no distortion caused by irregularities on the surface of the eye. Modern contact lenses are tiny pieces of a plastic-like substance that are shaped not only to correct the vision but also to fit the eye.

Most corrective glasses today are made with a coated plastic glass for safety. Often glasses can serve several purposes at once. This is most true of prescription sunglasses, which not only correct visual defects but also protect the eyes from the rays of the sun.

ALSO READ: EYE, GLASS, LENS, SIGHT.

GLENN, JOHN (born 1921) Cloudy skies and rain kept everyone waiting. Day after day, the weather at Cape Canaveral stayed bad. After nearly three weeks of rain, the weather finally changed. On February 20, 1962, John Glenn put on his spacesuit. He climbed into a small space capsule named *Friendship 7*. A few hours later, John Glenn became the first U.S. citizen to go into orbit in space.

John Herschel Glenn, Jr., was born in Cambridge, Ohio. He grew up in New Concord, Ohio, and joined the Marine Corps during World War II. In the Marines, he became a fighter pilot. In 1957, as a test pilot, Glenn flew a jet at speeds faster than sound from Los Angeles to New York. Two years later, he joined the Mercury space program as one of the original seven astronauts.

Friendship 7 orbited the Earth three times. After 4 hours and 55 minutes in space, Glenn splashed down safely in the Atlantic Ocean. He left the space program in 1964 and later became a businessman. Glenn was elected to the U.S. Senate from Ohio in 1974 and was reelected in 1980. In 1984 he failed to secure the Democratic nomination for the Presidency.

ALSO READ: ASTRONAUT, CAPE CANAVERAL, ROCKET, SPACE TRAVEL.

GLIDER Would you believe that people can fly in an aircraft that has no engine? A glider is a small, light (but heavier-than-air) aircraft without an engine. It gets its power from air currents that keep it aloft.

The first person-carrying glider that flew successfully was built and flown by Otto Lilienthal in 1891. It was so light that he could carry it himself. It looked like a big bat. It had two armrests, like crutches, which he could hold. He would hang from the center of the glider and run down a hill into the wind until the air currents lifted the glider into the air. He controlled it by shifting his body backward and forward and from side to side.

Modern gliders have controls, like airplanes. Most have standard airplane instruments, such as an airspeed indicator and a *variometer* (to measure the rate of climb or descent). *Spoilers* (pieces attached to the top of the wings with hinges) provide better control while landing, because they can be raised, to "spoil" the lifting force and increase the drag, or resistance.

Gliders are "launched" by being pulled by a cable attached to an automobile, or "towed" aloft by a cable attached to an airplane. This gives the glider enough speed to take off. Once aloft, it unhooks and is free to climb on the air currents.

The most efficient gliders are called *sailplanes*. They are extremely light with very long, slender wings. The wingspan varies from 60 to 80 feet (18–24 m). A good sailplane pilot can "soar" aloft for hours by using updrafts, or *thermals*. A thermal is a mass of warm air that rises from the ground because hot air always moves upward in colder air. The heated air exerts an upward force on the sailplane. This force is greater than the gravity that would pull the sailplane downward, so the sailplane

▲ *John Glenn, the first U.S. astronaut to go into orbit around the Earth, and more recently a prominent Democratic senator.*

▼ *"To design a flying machine is nothing; to build it is not much; to test it is everything," wrote Otto Lilienthal, the most famous glider-builder of the 19th century. While Lilienthal was at work in Germany, Octave Chanute was building and testing gliders in the United States. His biplane glider, shown here, looked more like an airplane than a glider.*

▼ *Glider pilots can feel free from the earth as their aircraft move up and down on air currents independent of engines.*

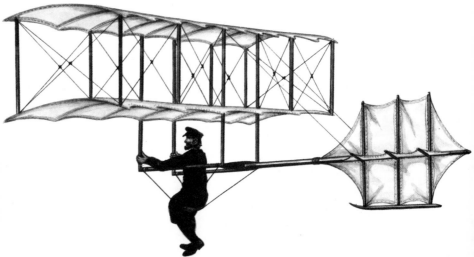

Goats are such surefooted animals that they can be trained to walk across a tightrope. They can even turn around on the rope without falling.

stays aloft. It will do so as long as the upward air current is more forceful than the "falling rate."

Although gliders are used mainly for sport, they can serve several other purposes. Both Germany and the Allies used gliders to transport troops and equipment during World War II. Today, gliders are often used for studying weather conditions and in testing new airplane designs.

ALSO READ: AIRPLANE, AVIATION, HANG GLIDING.

GLOSSARY see DICTIONARY.

GOAT A goat is a mammal that is closely related to the sheep. Goats can be wild or domestic. They are raised for milk, meat, wool, and skins. Goats are also kept as pets by children in some parts of the world.

Wool goats are common in the southwestern part of the United States, as well as in the Middle East. The thick wool of these goats is of fine quality. *Angora* goats produce wool for mohair. *Cashmere* goats' wool is used in fine, soft, expensive cashmere clothing. Goatskins are used for leather, such as fine Morocco leather.

Milk goats are of two types. Some, with pointed, stand-up ears, are *Swiss* goats. Toggenburg goats in the United States are of this type. Other milk goats, those with droopy ears,

are called *Nubian* goats. Goat's milk is sweet, rich, and nourishing. It has greater protein and fat than cow's milk and is also easier to digest than cow's milk. Goat's milk is commonly used by people in many countries outside the United States. Because goats can live on poorer grazing land than cows can, they are often raised in countries that have poor, dry land, unsuitable for cows. Good cheese can be made from goat's milk.

Goats chew the cud, like cattle. They have *cloven* hoofs. This means they have two toes and walk on their nails. Young goats can run and jump soon after birth. Both male and female adults have beards. A male is called a *buck* (nicknamed "billy"), a female is a *doe* (nicknamed "nanny"), and a young goat is a *kid*.

Wild goats live in rocky country in parts of Europe, Asia, and Africa. The wild Rocky Mountain goat of the United States and Canada is not a true goat but, like the true goat, it is related to the antelope. It is a stocky, high-shouldered animal with a long face and beard. Its thick, yellowish white coat is like the coat of a wool goat. It has short, curved black horns. The Rocky Mountain goat always lives above the tree line in the mountains, feeding on mosses, lichens, and bushes. It can climb steep rock faces without losing its foothold.

ALSO READ: MAMMAL.

▼ *The Rocky Mountain goat (left) from North America and the chamois from Europe are two members of the goat–antelope family. They live on opposite sides of the Atlantic Ocean, but have many similarities. Both are sturdy animals with extremely strong legs.*

GOBI DESERT How would you like to live where temperatures drop to –60° F (–51° C) in the winter and rise to 150° F (65° C) in the summer? Where icy winds blow in the winter and sandstorms howl in the summer? Where the average rainfall is only 5–8 inches (13–20 cm) a year, but when it does rain it pours down in heavy torrents? This is what it is like in the Gobi Desert! The Chinese call it the "sand desert."

You can understand why very few people live there. The Gobi has an area of about 500,000 square miles (about 1,300,000 sq. km), more than three times the size of California. It covers parts of the Mongolian People's Republic and the People's Republic of China. A highway and a railroad run across the Gobi, connecting Ulan Bator, Mongolia, with Chining, China. Camel caravans cross the desert in summer.

A few Mongolian tribes live in scattered grassy areas on the fringes of the desert. They wander from one grassland to another, grazing their goats, sheep, and cattle.

ALSO READ: DESERT, MONGOLIA.

GODDARD, ROBERT H. (1882–1945) The Goddard Space Flight Center in Greenbelt, Maryland, was named for Robert Hutchings Goddard. Along with the Russian physicist Konstantin Tsiolkovsky (1857–1935), he is widely regarded as the "Father of Modern Rocketry." His work helped lead to the development of intercontinental missiles and the U.S. space program.

Goddard was born in Worcester, Massachusetts. In 1914, he began to teach physics at Clark University in Worcester. There Goddard continued rocketry experiments he had started in college. He believed that a rocket could be built to travel into outer space. At first, Goddard used his salary to do research. Later, the Smithsonian Institution in Washington, D.C., gave him money.

By 1926, Goddard was ready to try his great experiment. He wanted to prove that a rocket could be powered by liquid fuel. Goddard's rocket stood only 10 feet (3 m) high, but it blasted up 180 feet (55 m) from a field near Auburn, Massachusetts.

Goddard moved to New Mexico where he could build bigger rockets. These new, larger rockets went thousands of feet into the air. In 1935, a Goddard rocket broke the speed of sound. He continued to work on rockets until his death.

ALSO READ: ROCKET.

GODS AND GODDESSES Do you know why the sun rises and sets? Do you know what lightning is? Can you explain the tides?

People who lived thousands of years ago asked themselves these questions. But they did not have enough scientific knowledge to explain the world around them. The moon and stars seemed to move across the sky at night, and the sun moved by day. Thunder roared, and lightning flashed. Grass, flowers, and crops sprang from the ground, flourished, and withered. Ancient peoples believed that some mighty power must cause all these things, so they invented gods and goddesses (*deities*) to explain them.

The gods and goddesses most familiar to us were those of the ancient Greeks and Romans. According to the Greeks, the gods lived on Mount Olympus, a high and majestic mountain. The gods were all related to each other, just like a human family. In fact, they had all the traits and habits (both good and bad) of *mortals* (human beings), but also they had miraculous powers.

The gods and goddesses looked like mortals, but they were larger,

▲ *The sands of the Gobi Desert are constantly shifting and changing shape.*

▼ *Robert Goddard in the 1930's, about to fire one of his liquid-fuel rockets. He was ridiculed during his lifetime, but today he and the Russian Konstantin Tsiolkovsky are regarded as the "fathers" of rocketry.*

GREEK AND ROMAN GODS AND GODDESSES		
Title	Greek	Roman
Leader of the Gods	Zeus	Jupiter (Jove)
Goddess of Marriage	Hera	Juno
God of the Sea and Waters	Poseidon	Neptune
God of the Underworld	Hades, Pluto	Dis, Orcus
God of the Sun	Apollo	Apollo
God of War	Ares	Mars
God of Fire	Hephaestus	Vulcan
God of Love	Eros	Cupid
Goddess of Love and Beauty	Aphrodite	Venus
Goddess of the Moon and Hunting	Artemis	Diana
Goddess of Wisdom	Athena	Minerva
Goddess of Corn and Fruit (Agriculture)	Demeter	Ceres
Goddess of the Hearth	Hestia	Vesta
God of Wine	Dionysus	Bacchus
Messenger of the Gods	Hermes	Mercury

▲ *The head of Zeus, shown on a coin. Zeus was the most important of the Greek gods. When he was taken into Roman myth, he was renamed Jupiter.*

▲ *Head of a bronze statue of Neptune in a museum in Athens.*

▲ *Aphrodite, the most beautiful of all the Greek goddesses. In Roman myths, she was called Venus.*

and most of them were exceptionally beautiful. Some of the deities could change their shapes into anything they wished. They had a magical food called *ambrosia* and a wine called *nectar*, both of which made them *immortal* (not able to die).

The deities were not solemn or dull. On the contrary, they were high-spirited, and enjoyed music, contests, and playing tricks. They were extremely jealous of each other and quarreled frequently. Although their life on Olympus was as pleasant as could be wished, they thoroughly enjoyed getting involved in the lives of mortals, and they often did. The Olympians could be very kind or very cruel. It was a foolish mortal who would dare to offend the gods, because the gods might punish any mortal who angered them.

The Gods of Olympus Zeus was the greatest of the gods, the wisest and most powerful of all. When Zeus was angry, he would stretch out his hand and hurl thunderbolts! His wife was Hera, goddess of marriage. Many of the other deities were sons and daughters of Zeus. One daughter, Athena, was goddess of wisdom. The city of Athens was in her care, and great temples were built in her honor. Artemis, another daughter of Zeus,

was moon goddess and goddess of hunting. She was the twin sister of Apollo, the sun god, who drove the chariot of the sun across the sky each day.

Two sons of Zeus were Ares, god of war, and Hermes, the messenger of the gods. Hermes wore a winged hat and winged sandals, and was very swift. Aphrodite, goddess of love and beauty, was the fairest of the goddesses. Her son was Eros, god of love.

Poseidon was Zeus's brother. He was god of all the waters and usually lived in a golden palace under the sea. Hestia, sister of Zeus, was goddess of home and hearth.

The only ugly god on Mount Olympus was Hephaestus, god of fire. He was a blacksmith and made armor for the gods. The mischievous god of wine, Dionysus, wandered about the world causing trouble. Demeter, goddess of corn and fruit, had the power to make the earth bloom or wither. Hades, or Pluto, ruled the land of the dead. Later, Hades came to be the name of the land of the dead itself.

Besides the Olympians, the Greeks invented many other lesser gods and magical beings. The Nymphs were goddesses of woods and fields, ruled over by Pan. Pan was the god of pastures, forests, and flocks. He is usually depicted as an animal-like figure with horns, a goat's beard, a crooked nose, pointed ears, a tail, and goat's feet. The reed pipe he played hypnotized people into following him and dancing in the fields. Pan may have contributed to the modern-day picture of the devil.

The Muses were the goddesses of the arts (music, dancing, literature, etc.), and the Graces were goddesses of beauty and charm. The Fates spun the thread of life, measured it, and cut it. They wielded great power over mortals from birth to death.

These gods and goddesses were very important to the Greeks. Since each deity ruled over some specific part of the world or human lives, a person would worship a particular god or goddess, depending on the specific problem or situation the person was concerned with. If someone wanted a good crop, he or she would bring offerings to the temple of Demeter. A person seeking protection during an ocean voyage would pray to Poseidon, who had the power to calm the waves.

All ancient peoples, including the Egyptians, Scandinavians, and Chinese, had their gods and goddesses. The areas of life over which they ruled were sometimes similar to those of the Greek deities. Gods in the various cultures differed mostly in the names that were given to them. For example, when the powerful Romans conquered Greece, they simply adopted the Greek gods for their own, changing some of their names. For example, Zeus was changed to Jupiter.

Gods and Goddesses Today What do these ancient gods and goddesses have to do with the world we live in today? People have always enjoyed stories about gods and lesser magical beings. We still read these marvelous tales today. They are called *myths*.

The ancient gods have survived in the names of the planets, months, and days of the week. They have also given us many of the words we use every day. Our word "volcano" comes from the name of the Roman god of fire, Vulcan. "Cereal" is named after Ceres, the Roman goddess of agriculture. Can you add any to the list below?

God or Goddess	*Word*
Mercury	mercurial
Mars	martial
Juno	Junoesque
Bellona (a Roman war goddess)	bellicose, belligerent
Titans	titanic

ALSO READ: ANDROMEDA, DAY OF THE WEEK, FATES, FURY, GREEK LITERATURE, HOMER, MONTH, MUSE, MYTHOLOGY, NORSE MYTHS.

GOLD Rings and lockets are often made of gold. It is a yellow metal with a beautiful luster, or shine. Gold has always been valuable to people, partly because it is scarce. But gold is also soft and easy to shape. It does not rust and is not affected by most acids.

Because of its softness, gold must be mixed with other metals, such as

▼ *Panning for gold in a streambed. Light material is washed out, leaving behind any grains of gold.*

▲ *Horus, an ancient Egyptian god of the sun. He had the head of a hawk.*

▲ *Agni, Hindu god of fire. He is said to have been born when two pieces of wood were rubbed together.*

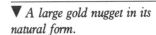

▼ *A large gold nugget in its natural form.*

▲ *Bars of gold stacked in a bank vault.*

Most of the nation's gold is stored in underground vaults at Fort Knox, Kentucky. In 1986 there were more than 9,000 tons (8,100 metric tons) of the precious metal in store—heavier than 5,000 family automobiles. A cubic foot (0.03 m³) of gold weighs half a ton (450 kg)—heavier than 7 men.

The biggest gold nugget ever found weighed about 472 pounds (214 kg). It was discovered in New South Wales, Australia, in 1872. When refined, it yielded about 187 pounds (85 kg) of pure gold.

copper, platinum, or nickel, to make jewelry and coins. These other metals, when mixed with gold, are called *alloys*. Look inside a gold ring. Is there a stamp, such as "14k"? The k stands for *karat*, a measure of the amount of gold in the ring. Since pure gold is 24 karat, a "14k" ring contains 14 parts of gold and 10 parts of an alloy. (Sometimes the word is spelled *carat*, shortened to "ct.")

Gold is found in the earth primarily in three ways. *Lode* (or vein) *deposits* are layers of rock in the earth's crust that contain gold. *Placer deposits* are grains of gold (often called *nuggets*) that are found in streambeds. Seawater contains about 10 million tons (9 million metric tons) of gold, although no efficient way to remove it has yet been found.

People have found many uses for gold. Gold coins have been used as money throughout history. Until 1934, the United States (like most other countries) was on the *gold standard*, which meant that paper money could be traded in for a certain amount of gold. Dentists may use gold to make fillings for teeth because acids in the mouth do not affect it. Gold is also beaten into thin, nearly transparent sheets called *gold leaf*, which is used for decorative work.

ALSO READ: ALCHEMY, CHEMISTRY, DENTISTRY, EL DORADO, FORT KNOX, GOLD RUSH, JEWELRY.

GOLDEN FLEECE see JASON.

GOLD RUSH Gold has been mined for thousands of years. But it has been found only in limited amounts and in only a few parts of the world. The discovery of a new source of gold usually sets off a "gold rush" as people flock to the area to join in the search.

One of the biggest gold rushes of all time occurred in California in the

1800's. In 1848, large quantities of gold were discovered at the sawmill of John A. Sutter near San Francisco. By 1849 the gold rush was on. Thousands of people from all over the United States went to California. Ministers left their churches to go West. Grocers, doctors, blacksmiths, bookkeepers, and others headed for the gold fields. They became known as the "forty-niners." Although many never found the riches they dreamed about, they helped to settle the U.S. West.

In the gold fields, the miners (or *prospectors*) lived in tents and shacks. Their camps had descriptive names, such as Hangtown or Rough-and-Ready. The land belonged to whoever arrived first. Each miner would stake his "claim," or area of ground, and start digging. American Indians, Spaniards, Mexicans, Chinese, and people of many other nationalities staked their claims. The city of San Francisco prospered at first from the gold rush. But as more people left for the gold camps, the streets became deserted.

Some of the newcomers grew rich without going to the gold fields. They opened stores and sold clothing, tools, and food. Prices soared as the demand increased. An egg cost as much as a dollar. The miners who found gold had to spend much of it just to live. Sacks of gold were often used in place of money. Outlaws flocked to the mining camps. They stole gold, killed prospectors, and "jumped," or seized, claims. There were no police, and every person made his own laws. Some order was restored after 1850 when California became a state of the Union.

Another wild and famous gold rush began in 1896 when quantities of gold were discovered along the Klondike Creek in the Yukon River Valley of Alaska and Canada. Thousands of men braved the frozen north, hoping to get rich.

Several writers spent some time in

the gold camps. Mark Twain and Bret Harte wrote colorful and amusing stories about prospectors in California. Jack London wrote a well-known book, *Call of the Wild*. It tells about the terrible hardships of the Yukon prospectors and of a courageous sled dog. Robert Service wrote some stirring poems about the Yukon gold rush.

ALSO READ: CALIFORNIA; GOLD; LONDON, JACK; OUTLAW; TWAIN, MARK; YUKON TERRITORY.

GOLF Have you ever hit a pebble with a stick? Shepherds in the fields have done this for centuries with their staffs or crooks. About 500 years ago in Scotland, the game of golf was devised by substituting a small ball for the pebble, and by making better clubs to hit the ball. Golf has become a sport popular with men, women, boys, and girls. Many expert golfers are professionals, who earn their living playing golf. Some of them make hundreds of thousands of dollars each year. Nonprofessional (amateur) golfers play for fun and sport. Strength is helpful in golf, but more important are experience and good coordination, as well as good technique.

Golf is played on a *course* consisting of 18 holes. A golf hole is made up of a *tee* (a small, flat, grassy area), a *fairway* (a long stretch of mowed grass), and a *green* (a closely mowed grassy area). Each hole may range from 100 to 600 yards (90–550 m) in length. A typical 18-hole golf course is usually about 6,000 to 7,000 yards (5.5–6.4 km) in length. In every green on a course is a hole, 4¼ inches (11 cm) in diameter, called the *cup*. A *round* of golf consists of playing 18 holes on a course (called a *links* in some places) in correct, consecutive order. Golf is generally played in groups of two to four persons.

On each tee, beginning with the first, the golfer places his or her ball

on a small wooden or plastic peg, also called a tee. Using a long, slender club, the golfer hits the ball, or *tees off*, trying to drive the ball straight and far down the fairway. If the person *hooks* his or her drive and hits to the left (playing right-handed), the ball may end up in the *rough*, an area with tall grass, rocks, and trees that borders the fairway on each side. The golfer may also go into the rough if he or she *slices* (hits the ball so that it veers to the right). The golfer then makes a few more shots, finally hitting the ball onto the green. If the person is not careful, the ball may go into a *sand trap* (or *bunker*) before it reaches the green. Once on the green, the golfer tries to *putt* the ball (hit it much more gently than in driving) into the cup in the green. Sticking out of the cup is a long pole with a colored flag at its top. The flag, with a number identifying the hole, shows the golfers where the cup is and helps them to aim their shots properly.

Golf Rules and Equipment In golf, each time a player hits the ball with a club, it counts as a stroke. Even if a golfer misses the ball, he or she is still charged with a stroke. The object of the game is to finish each hole in as few strokes as possible. The golfer with the lowest number of strokes is the winner. Each hole has a number of strokes called *par*. Par for a hole is usually three, four, or five strokes. A good golfer may make par for each

▲ *Miners searching for gold in California during the gold rush that started in 1848–1849. Some miners dug into the ground and others panned for gold in streams.*

▼ *A golfer has just completed his swing, and the ball is on its way to the green, and hopefully the hole.*

▶ *The delicate art of putting is just as important to mastery in the game of golf as the swing.*

Golf clubs are sometimes called by strange names. A No. 2 wood may be called a *brassie*; a No. 3 wood, a *spoon*; a No. 4 wood, a *baffie*; and a No. 5 iron, a *mashie*.

▲ *Mikhail Gorbachev, Soviet head of state since 1985. Since coming to power he has made many reforms. In 1987, Gorbachev visited Washington, D.C. for a summit meeting with President Reagan. At this meeting a treaty was signed to reduce strategic nuclear weapons. It was called the Intermediate Nuclear Forces (INF) Treaty.*

hole, a *birdie* (one stroke below par), an *eagle* (two strokes below par), or an *albatross* or *double eagle* (three strokes below par), or even a *hole-in-one* (one stroke from tee to cup). An average golfer may make a *bogey* (one stroke over par for the hole), a *double bogey* (two strokes over par), or worse. Par for a course is the total of the par scores for the course's holes.

In addition to a supply of small, hard, white golf balls, the player must have an assortment of no more than 14 clubs. Different clubs are used, depending on the distance to the hole, the direction of the wind, and the particular skill of the player. A set of golf clubs consists of four *woods* (with wooden heads), used for long shots; eight *irons* (with iron or aluminum heads), used for shorter shots; a *wedge* (a special iron); and a *putter*, used on the green. The clubs' heads have different sloping *faces* (sides) to vary the distance and height a golfer can achieve on a shot.

Some players hire *caddies* to carry their clubs for them. Others use lightweight, two-wheeled, hand-pulled carts to carry their clubs. Small, motorized golf carts take players and their clubs around many golf courses today.

ALSO READ: SPORTS; SPORTS, PROFESSIONAL.

GORBACHEV, MIKHAIL SERGEYEVICH (born 1931) Mikhail Gorbachev was born in Stavropol Kray, Russia. His parents were peasants working on a state collective farm. He left home to study in Moscow, and became a member of the Communist Party—a necessary step in the Soviet Union for anyone seeking advancement. He began to rise through the party ranks.

He first came to prominence in 1978, when he became a member of the Secretariat of the Central Committee of the Communist Party. In 1980 he became a member of the more select Politburo. During the administration of Yuri Andropov (1982–1984), Gorbachev was picked out by observers as one of the younger and more energetic Soviet leaders. On the death of Andropov, and the succession of the elderly Konstantin Chernenko, Gorbachev's future seemed bright.

Chernenko died in 1985 and, at the comparatively young age of 54, Gorbachev took over. He set a new style of Soviet leadership. Other world leaders noted his sharp mind and toughness in negotiation. His 1985 summit meeting with U.S. President Ronald Reagan was the first between heads of state from the two superpowers for six years.

ALSO READ: SOVIET UNION.

GORGON The myths of ancient Greece tell about three hideous monsters called Gorgons. These monsters were sisters named Medusa, Euryale, and Stheno. They had huge wings, horrible staring eyes, and writhing snakes about their heads instead of hair. Medusa was the most terrible of the three. Anyone who looked directly into her eyes turned to stone. Her sisters were immortal (they could not die). But Medusa was killed by a brave hero named Perseus. He cut off her head while looking at her in a mirror. Pegasus, the winged horse of Greek myth, arose from her blood. Perseus later used the head to turn his enemies to stone.

ALSO READ: MYTHOLOGY.

GOTHIC ARCHITECTURE

Of all buildings, those in the Gothic style are among the most beautiful. In Europe, Gothic architecture lasted as a style of building from the late 1100's to the 1500's. Gothic architects used *vertical* (up-and-down) lines to reach for the sky. They also wanted their buildings to look light and delicate. To create a feeling of lightness, they did away with the heavy walls used in earlier structures. To open up enclosed spaces, they used large windows of stained glass and *tracery* (frames of stone that held the glass). Inside Gothic churches the pillars were very high and thin. Pointed arches were used for doors and windows, and the ceilings were *vaulted* (made of arched stonework). Towers also added height to Gothic structures.

Heaven is described in the Bible as a place of gold and jewels, shimmering in the sunlight. Stained-glass windows and elaborate carvings were used to make Gothic churches look like heaven on Earth.

To keep the thin pillars and high vaults from collapsing, Gothic architects invented the *flying buttress*. A *buttress* is a heavy mass of stone that braces a wall. To allow low aisles to be built, buttresses were set outside a church and connected to its center part with *flyers*, rigid arches that transmitted the forces to the buttresses. Flying buttresses cast weblike shadows that make Gothic churches seem lacy. Since the walls did not have to bear much weight, there was room for large stained-glass windows, set in decorative tracery.

Most of the famous churches in Europe were built during the Middle Ages. The cathedral at Rheims, France, is one of the finest examples of Gothic architecture. Begun in 1211, it was the church where the

▲ *This ancient Greek carving shows how ugly a Gorgon was! She had snakes on her head instead of hair. However, later Greek artists showed the Gorgons as beautiful.*

▼ *The nave of Exeter Cathedral, England. The cathedral was built early in the 12th century, and extensively rebuilt during the 13th century. Although it suffered bomb damage during World War II, it still stands today as a fine example of Gothic architecture.*

▼ *A section through a Gothic church, showing how the structure is supported, or* buttressed.

Flying buttress

Buttress

▲ *A lofty spire of the Cathedral of Notre Dame, in Paris, France, rises gracefully behind a foreground of stained-glass windows. The cathedral is one of the most impressive surviving examples of Gothic architecture.*

▲ *Strange monsterlike creatures, called* gargoyles, *decorate many Gothic cathedrals. Most gargoyles simply cover up drainage pipes.*

French kings were crowned. Houses and commercial buildings were also done in the Gothic style. Gothic palaces were elegant with paint and carving, towers and gateways. Half-timbered houses, whose heavy frames showed, were less elegant but had a vivid, interesting look of their own. The Gothic style was revived in the 1800's by the Victorians, who admired it for its religious intensity.

ALSO READ: ARCHITECTURE, CATHEDRAL, STAINED GLASS.

GOVERNMENT Imagine thousands of people living and working together with no rules or rulers. There would be complete confusion without any system of organization. So many people would have different ideas about how to do things that arguments would go on constantly. Nothing could be done successfully. It is easy to see why some form of ruling system is necessary. Governing bodies come in all sizes—from a small student council in a school to the U.S. Congress (100 senators and 435 representatives).

Government is control by a person or a group of persons having the power to make and enforce laws. The government of a country must control national laws, finances, trade, relations with foreign governments, and other matters that affect the entire nation. Governments vary in different parts of the world according to the culture and traditions of the people they rule. Countries with complete independence are said to be *sovereign*. Any ruler, such as a king or dictator, who has complete authority over his people, also has sovereignty.

No two forms of national government are exactly alike. Most systems of government today fall under two headings—*democratic* forms of government and *totalitarian* forms of government. *Democracy* is a system of government in which the people take an active part by voting for their

FORMS OF GOVERNMENT	
System	*Rule by*
Anarchy	Harmony, without law
Aristocracy	A privileged order
Autocracy	One man, absolutely
Bureaucracy	Officials
Democracy	The people
Diarchy	Two rulers or authorities
Ergatocracy	The workers
Ethnocracy	Race or ethnic group
Gerontocracy	Elders
Matriarchy	A mother (or mothers)
Meritocracy	The most able
Monarchy	Hereditary head of state
Oligarchy	Small exclusive class
Patriarchy	Male head of family
Plutocracy	The wealthy
Technocracy	Technical experts
Theocracy	Divine guidance

leaders, and by electing others in their place if they believe they have failed. *Totalitarianism* is a system in which one group or even one person (or dictator) has complete control over the people in a country.

The United States has a *representative democracy* (or *republic*). The people elect a President, congressional representatives, and other officials to represent them in positions of leadership. The U.S. government is divided into three branches. The *legislative* branch (Congress) makes the laws. The *executive* branch proposes and enforces the laws and manages the affairs of state. The *judicial* branch decides whether or not laws are constitutional—not contrary to principles in the U.S. Constitution. All branches of government must perform their duties within the limits described in the Constitution.

Countries such as Great Britain, Japan, and Sweden are also representative democracies with basic laws, basic freedoms, and elections. Elected representatives sit in legislative assemblies similar to our Congress. For traditional reasons, however, these three nations still have monarchs who serve as advisers and have no real power. These countries are also called *constitutional* (or *limited*) *monarchies.*

In ancient times, several tribes would often gather together and choose a strong ruler. When the ruler died, a son, or another member of the family, usually took his or her place. Most of these rulers had absolute control over their people. *Absolute monarchs* have been known by various titles. They would be *kings* or *queens* in Europe, *emperors* in ancient Rome, *sultans* in Arabia, *pharaohs* in ancient Egypt, and *czars* in Russia. But not all monarchs were absolute rulers. Religious leaders were often equally powerful, as were the nobles. Both these groups often took part in the governing of countries through the centuries.

If the government of a country is controlled by a few families of noble birth, it is called an *aristocracy*. If a country is ruled by a small group of people, the government is called an *oligarchy*. Some Latin American countries today are controlled by oligarchies. In an aristocracy or an oligarchy, the land and wealth belong to a few people. Most peasants and

▲ *The parliament of King Edward I of England in about 1275. Edward brought about many government reforms. He encouraged the development of parliament, and worked against the old system of feudalism.*

▼ *Prime Minister Winston Churchill, head of the British government, uses the radio on May 8, 1945, to tell the people the great news that World War II in Europe has ended in victory over Germany.*

workers are very poor.

Another form of government that has been common in Latin American countries is *military dictatorship*. The leader, or *dictator*, supported by the armed forces, has complete power. In many cases, dictators have seized that power by revolution. They control countries by force and destroy any opposition to their policies. They prohibit freedom of speech, of religion, and of the press. Two major dictators of the 20th century were Adolf Hitler in Germany and Benito Mussolini in Italy. Dictatorships are one form of totalitarian government.

Many *Communist* governments are totalitarian. One political party dominates, and, although elections are held, the people have only one candidate to vote for. The government has strong control over the daily lives of the people. The press is government-controlled, and political opposition must be carried on in secret. Some countries, however, have had democratically elected Communist governments.

Besides national governments, which run the entire country, most nations also have smaller units of government. In the United States, the citizens of a state elect governors and state legislators to deal with state problems. The citizens of a city elect mayors and city council members to handle city matters. The Russian system has a *soviet*, or council, at each level of government.

Governments may differ, but,

In the United States, over 13 million people—about a sixth of the nation's workers—work for the government or for state or municipal authorities. The U.S. government is the nation's largest employer.

▲ *Ronald Reagan, 40th President of the United States.*

▲ *Kenneth Grahame, the British author of* The Wind in the Willows *and other popular books.*

whenever a group of people—a family or a nation—are gathered together, some form of government is essential.

For further information on:

Branches of Government, *see* CABINET, UNITED STATES; CONGRESS, UNITED STATES; FEDERAL BUREAU OF INVESTIGATION; LAW; LEGISLATURE; LOCAL GOVERNMENT; PARLIAMENT; POLITICAL PARTY; STATE GOVERNMENT.

Government Buildings, *see* CAPITOL, UNITED STATES; KREMLIN; WHITE HOUSE.

Government Documents, *see* BILL OF RIGHTS; CONSTITUTION, UNITED STATES; MAGNA CARTA.

Government Offices, *see* KINGS AND QUEENS, PRESIDENCY, PRIME MINISTER, PRINCES AND PRINCESSES, VICE-PRESIDENT.

Political Philosophers, *see* LENIN, NIKOLAI; MACHIAVELLI, NICCOLO; MARX, KARL; PLATO.

Symbols of Government, *see* CROWN JEWELS, FLAG, NATIONAL ANTHEM, STAR-SPANGLED BANNER.

Types of Government, *see* CHURCH AND STATE, COMMUNISM, DEMOCRACY, DICTATOR, FASCISM, FEUDALISM, MONARCHY, REPUBLIC, SOCIALISM.

GRAFTING see PLANT BREEDING.

GRAHAME, KENNETH (1859–1932) Kenneth Grahame was the author of a beloved book for children, *The Wind in the Willows* (1908). He was born in Edinburgh, Scotland, and spent part of his early life in a small fishing village not far from there. He became a clerk for the Bank of England after attending Oxford University. Grahame began to write children's stories in his spare time. Two collections of stories for children, *The Golden Age* (1895) and *Dream Days* (1898), were published. He married in 1899. He and his wife had one son, named Alastair.

The enormously popular *Wind in the Willows* was started in the form of letters to his son. Before leaving on a vacation, Alastair asked his father to send him regular installments of bedtime stories. Grahame did so, and thus the first chapters of the book were created. *The Wind in the Willows* tells the humorous adventures of a number of small animals. Kenneth Grahame retired from banking after *The Wind in the Willows* became famous, and he lived the rest of his life in the country.

ALSO READ: CHILDREN'S LITERATURE.

GRAIN Grain is the edible seed, or *kernel*, of certain grasses. These grasses are usually called *cereal grains*, or *cereals*. Grain has been an important food for people and animals for thousands of years.

Long ago, people in several different areas of the world learned how to cultivate wild cereal grains and domesticate wild animals. They built villages in regions where cereals and animals thrived best.

Today, more than half the world's croplands are used for cereal grains. The cereals are inexpensive to grow, and grain can be dried and stored for long periods. Grain is the most frequently eaten food in many parts of the world. It contains carbohydrates, protein, fat, and B vitamins.

The most commonly grown grains are wheat, corn, rice, barley, rye, and oats. Wheat is considered the most important of all grain crops. It is grown and made into flour in most countries of the world. The largest wheat crops come from the United States, Canada, the Soviet Union, and Europe. Corn (sometimes called maize) is grown in large quantities in the United States, China, South America, and southern Europe. Rice is a principal food in China, Japan, and India. Barley, rye, and oats are grown in smaller quantities around the globe.

All the grains can be milled into flour. Wheat and rye are used mostly for making bread. Many of the grains are made into "breakfast cereals." Margarine, cooking oil, and syrup are processed from corn. Oats are eaten by people mainly in the form of oatmeal. Barley is used for making whiskey and beer. Whiskey is also made from rye, barley, and corn. Grain is used in the manufacture of antibiotic drugs and vitamins. All the grains are widely used as feed for cattle and other livestock.

After most cereals have been har-vested, they must be *threshed* to sepa-rate the grain from the plant. This process is carried out by machines today. Grain is then stored in silos and grain elevators before being shipped to processing plants.

ALSO READ: ALCOHOLIC BEVERAGE, AN-TIBIOTIC, CORN, FLOUR MAKING, RICE, WHEAT.

GRAMMAR *And ate butter Don jelly peanut sandwiches three.* When you make sense of that "sentence," you show that you understand what grammar is about.

Language, whether it is spoken or written, is used by people to commu-nicate their ideas. Usually these ideas are expressed in sentences made up of words. Although each word has its own meaning or meanings, we can't just string together a lot of words and expect them to make sense to others. Words must be arranged in special ways to make sentences that can be understood. The study of the ways in which words are formed and arranged to make sentences is called grammar.

Words work in a number of ways to communicate ideas. In the study of grammar, words are usually classified

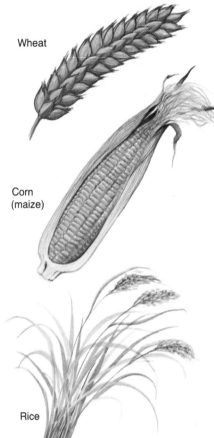

Wheat

Corn (maize)

Rice

▲ *Wheat, corn (maize), and rice are three of the world's major grain crops. Wheat covers a larger area of farmland than any other food crop. Corn is important in warm, humid areas, especially in Africa and Asia, and is widely grown in the United States. Rice is the basic food for about one-half of the world's people.*

◄ *Turkish women harvesting ripe wheat.*

GRAMMAR

How many grammatical sentences can you make out of this sentence: *The black cat with the white tail chased the white dog with the black tail.* The second sentence could be: *The white dog with the white tail chased the black cat with the black tail.* There are eight possible sentences in all.

as *parts of speech* according to what they do in a sentence. The four main classes of words are: *nouns* (including pronouns), *verbs*, *adjectives*, and *adverbs*. Other words, referred to as *function words* because of what they do or the *function* they perform in a sentence, are called by such names as determiners, prepositions, conjunctions, auxiliaries, subordinators, relatives, intensifiers, and sentence-starters. Whatever system of grammar is taught, it is important if you are studying the English language to understand what role each word plays in the arrangement of a sentence. The arrangement of words in a sentence is known as *syntax*.

Don ate three peanut butter and jelly sandwiches.

Those are exactly the same words you read before, but the meaning is now clear because the words are arranged in a pattern that you, as a speaker of our language, are used to. You understand the sentence because you know not only the meaning of each of the words but also the meaning of *all* the words as they have been grouped together.

Most sentences have two parts. One part is called the *subject*. It tells what the sentence is about. The subject may be a noun or a pronoun. The other part of a sentence is called the *predicate*. It tells what is said about the subject or what the subject does. A predicate contains a verb. The verb may be alone, or it may have other words with it. For instance, it may include an adjective that describes the subject. The two parts of a sentence may appear in different places, depending on what the writer or speaker wishes to say and how he or she wishes to say it.

Mike was hungry. In this sentence, *Mike* is the subject. He is the person the sentence is about. *Was hungry* is the predicate, because it tells what the subject did or felt. *Was* is the verb. *Hungry* is the adjective that describes *Mike*, the subject.

Sentences not only have parts. They also have patterns. The four basic sentence patterns are:

(1) noun-verb (NV)
(2) noun-verb-noun (NVN)
(3) noun-linking verb-adjective (NLkVA)
(4) noun-verb-noun-noun (NVNN).

Every sentence fits one of these patterns (or a combination of two or more). Here are some examples.

1. Don ate. The subject, *Don*, did something. He ate, so *ate* is the verb. (NV)
2. Don ate sandwiches. *Don*, the subject, did something to an object. He *ate* sandwiches. *Sandwiches* is the object. (NVN)
3. Marian is thoughtful. This sentence has a linking verb, *is*, that connects the subject, *Marian*, with an adjective, *thoughtful*, which describes her. (NLkVA)
4. Schulz writes the comic strip *Peanuts*. The verb, *writes*, connects the subject, *Schulz*, with the other nouns, *comic strip* and *Peanuts*. (NVNN)

■ LEARN BY DOING

Look at these lines from Lewis Carroll's poem "Jabberwocky."

'Twas brillig, and the slithy toves
Did gyre and gimble in the wabe;
All mimsy were the borogoves,
And the mome raths outgrabe.

Notice how the "nonsense" words seem to make sense. This is because the *pattern* of the words is meaningful. Carroll seems to be telling you that there is meaning in certain arrangements of words even if the words have no meaning themselves. Notice that Carroll can't do without words like "the," "and," or "with." Can you explain this? Read some other nonsense poems by Carroll or any other poet you can find who seems to show what fun can be had in playing with words. ■

ALSO READ: PARTS OF SPEECH.

GRAND CANYON Perhaps the best way to see the Grand Canyon is between the ears of a mule. Every year thousands of visitors ride down the Bright Angel or the Kaibab Trail to the Colorado River at the bottom of the canyon, then up the opposite side. The Grand Canyon, located in northwestern Arizona, is one of nature's most spectacular creations.

The Colorado River is the "cutting edge" that has carved the Grand Canyon. Scientists believe that several million years ago, this area was pushed upward by the Earth's movement. Since then, the river and its tributaries have cut through many layers of rock to form the deep gorges that make up the Grand Canyon. Erosion from rain and wind has increased the size of the gorges. Some of them reach a depth of over 5,000 feet (about 1,500 m).

The north rim of the canyon is called the Kaibab Plateau, and the south rim is the Coconino Plateau.

▼ *The Grand Canyon, the world's largest gorge, was formed by the Colorado River cutting into its bed.*

The canyon itself is made up of many brightly colored cliffs, valleys, hills, and plateaus. The canyon walls reveal different layers, or *strata*, of rock. Each layer marks a different time in the Earth's history. The layers of rock at the bottom of the canyon are thought to have been formed more than one billion years ago. There are several distinct zones of plant and animal life along the walls of the gorges. The zone nearest the river has cactus, like a desert. The zone at the top has forest land with many spruce and fir trees.

Indians have lived in and around the Grand Canyon since at least the 1200's. One small tribe, the Havasupai, live today in a village at the bottom of the canyon.

The first white person to lead a party through the Grand Canyon in a boat was Major John Wesley Powell in 1869. The Grand Canyon National Park was established in 1919 and was later, in 1975, nearly doubled in size by an act of the U.S. Congress.

ALSO READ: ARIZONA, CANYON, EROSION, GEOLOGY.

GRANITE Granite is a hard rock composed mainly of quartz, feldspar, mica, and hornblende. It may be pink, light gray, dark gray, or one of several other colors.

All granite was once molten rock, like lava, that cooled and hardened deep below the Earth's surface. Most granite is coarse-grained—that is, the rock's crystals can be seen with the naked eye. Such granite cooled slowly, so that there was time for large crystals to form. However, some granite is fine-grained with tiny crystals. This granite cooled more quickly.

Granite is found in more than half of the states of the United States. It is cut or blasted out of *quarries* (deep pits). Granite is quarried in many other countries. Because it is heavy

The hike into the Grand Canyon down one side and out the other is almost 21 miles (34 km) long and takes most visitors two days to complete.

▲ *Granite makes a good building stone. Aberdeen, in Scotland, is called the Granite City because so many of its buildings are made using granite from a local quarry, Rubislaw. This is a granite public building in the older part of the city.*

and difficult to ship, granite is often used locally where it is found. It is valuable as a building stone because it is strong and durable, resisting all forms of weather. Granite also has a pleasing appearance. Many buildings, bridges, and monuments are made of granite. A red granite found in Finland can be beautifully polished and is used as a monument or cemetery stone. Vermont and New Hampshire, with their valuable granite deposits, have both been called the "Granite State," though New Hampshire has the nickname officially.

ALSO READ: BUILDING MATERIAL, QUARRYING, ROCK.

GRANT, ULYSSES SIMPSON

(1822–1885) After the Civil War, General Grant, who had led the Union armies to victory, was probably the most popular man in the Northern states. He was nominated by the Republican Party to run for President in 1868, and he won an easy victory in the election.

Grant had been a shy boy when he was growing up in southwestern Ohio. He was graduated from the United States Military Academy at West Point in 1843 and was assigned to several different army posts. He fought in the war against Mexico. He was promoted to the rank of captain

in 1853. Grant resigned from the Army in 1854 and then failed in several different lines of work. By the time the Civil War began, he had a wife and four children. Grant tried to support them on the 50 dollars a month he made selling in a leather shop in Galena, Illinois.

In his 30's, Grant considered himself a failure. But he wanted to fight for the Union. His opportunity came when the governor of his state appointed him colonel of a regiment of Illinois volunteers. He became a brigadier general within a few months. An officer of dogged determination, he won a series of brilliant victories. On one occasion, the commander of a Confederate fort asked on what terms Grant would accept his surrender. "No terms," was the reply, "except an unconditional and immediate surrender." Since Grant's initials were U.S., from then on he was known as "Unconditional Surrender Grant." On March 8, 1864, President Lincoln made him commander of all the Union forces. Grant helped bring the war to an end in little more than a year.

Grant had been a great soldier, but he showed poor judgment as President. He himself was honest, but some of those he appointed to high office were not. They caused financial difficulties for the government and the country. He was not blamed for

While Grant was president, Alexander Graham Bell invented the telephone (1876), General Custer and his men were massacred by Sioux and Cheyenne Indians at the Battle of Little Bighorn (1876), and the first transcontinental railroad was completed (1869).

ULYSSES SIMPSON GRANT
EIGHTEENTH PRESIDENT   MARCH 4, 1869–MARCH 4, 1877

Born: April 27, 1822, near Point Pleasant, Ohio
Parents: Jesse Root and Hannah Simpson Grant
Education: United States Military Academy, West Point, New York
Religion: Methodist
Occupation: Army officer
Political Party: Republican
Married: 1848, Julia Dent (1826–1902)
Children: 1 daughter, 3 sons
Died: Mount McGregor, New York (near Saratoga), July 23, 1885
Buried: Grant's Tomb, Riverside Drive, New York City

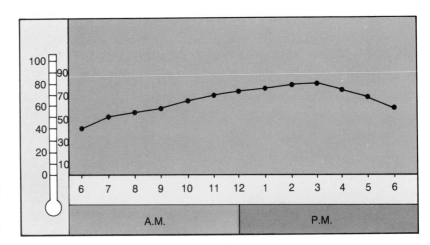

this, and was reelected as President in 1872. Grant's second term was marked by even greater "scandals" arising from dishonest acts by officials he had appointed.

Grant was not a good businessman. A few years after he left the White House, he lost most of his savings through investments in a company that went out of business. To provide for his family, he wrote his *Personal Memoirs*, which became a best-seller. He finished the manuscript only a few days before dying from cancer. Even those citizens who had blamed him for government corruption were moved to admiration.

ALSO READ: CIVIL WAR, MEXICAN WAR, RECONSTRUCTION.

GRAPH You have probably drawn a picture of a scene on a sunny day. You can imagine how hot it is when you look at your drawing. You can also make another type of "picture" that shows, not just one moment in a day, but how the temperature changes through the whole day in relation to the time. A graph can picture how these two things, time and temperature—or any other two things—are related. A graph makes it easy to see—not just to think of—the relationship between two subjects.

On this page is a simple *line graph* showing the temperature for each time of day on a certain day. A line is used to connect the points. The numerals along the horizontal *axis* (base line) tell what time of day it is, and are marked for every hour from 6:00 a.m. until 6:00 p.m. The numerals along the vertical axis tell the temperature. For example, to see what the temperature was at 11:00 a.m., locate 11:00 a.m. on the horizontal axis, and run your finger straight upwards to the point. Now, run your finger left to the vertical axis, and read the temperature. You will see that at 11:00 a.m., the temperature was 70° F (21° C).

The highest two dots—80° F (27° C)—are at 2:00 and 3:00 p.m., showing that that hour was the hottest of the day. The temperature was 60° F (15.5° C) at 9:00 a.m. and at 6:00 p.m., shown by the lowest points.

Another common kind of graph is the *bar graph*. In a bar graph, a heavy line, or *bar*, is used instead of a point. In the example shown here, the bar graph tells how many days each boy was absent from school. The horizontal axis lists the names of the boys, and the vertical axis lists numbers of days absent. For example, Bob was absent two days from school, since his bar only goes up two spaces. Larry's bar goes all the way to 7, so he was absent the most.

A third kind is the *picture graph*. This one can be fun to make. In it, each thing measured or counted is represented by one symbol. The symbols are pictures, not just dots.

▲ *An example of a simple line graph.*

▼ *An example of a bar graph.*

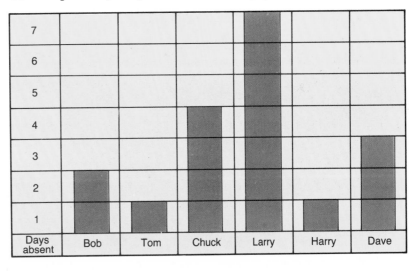

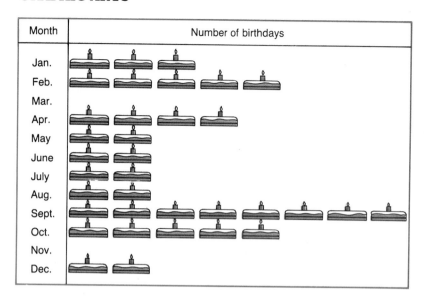

Month	Number of birthdays
Jan.	
Feb.	
Mar.	
Apr.	
May	
June	
July	
Aug.	
Sept.	
Oct.	
Nov.	
Dec.	

▲ *An example of a picture graph.*

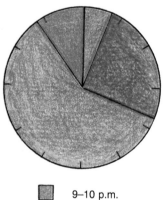

9–10 p.m.

After 10 p.m.

Before 8 p.m.

8–9 p.m.

▲ *A "pie" diagram showing the results of a survey of 40 children's bedtimes. Two went to bed before 8 p.m., 10 went to bed between 8 and 9 p.m., 24 went to bed between 9 and 10 p.m., and 4 went to bed after 10 p.m. The "pie" diagram, a type of graph, shows the proportions of children going to bed at different times.*

■ **LEARN BY DOING**

Make a list of the birthdays of your classmates. Then count how many are in each month.

Then you can make a picture graph of how many birthdays are in each month. You could use one cake to stand for each birthday, as in the graph shown here. When you draw the graph, make sure the figures are the same distance apart. Then you can tell at a glance which number is largest or smallest. ■

A fourth kind of graph is the *circle graph*, or *pie chart*. It is commonly used to show how the parts of something are related to the whole.

ALSO READ: MATHEMATICS.

GRAPHIC ARTS The different ways of making copies of pictures and books are called "graphic arts." The copies, or reproductions, are usually made up of lines and strokes rather than blocks of color (as in painting). Some people also consider drawing to be one of the graphic arts.

For many years, books were written and illustrated by hand. These books were beautifully made, but they were very expensive and few people could afford to buy them. Then people discovered a way to re-

produce the words and pictures of books. The letters and pictures of each page were carved on a flat block of wood. Ink was rolled over the wood. A sheet of paper was pressed onto the inked wood so that an impression in ink of the letters and pictures was left on the paper. This method was the earliest form of *printing*. Printers could make page after page from one block. Much later, in the 1400's, Johannes Gutenberg invented *movable type*, which allowed blocks to be made much more quickly. Today's books, magazines, and newspapers are printed on fast machines. The graphic artists who design and print them often make them as beautiful as the old hand-made books.

Other methods of printing are used by artists to produce pictures and designs known as *prints*. These pictures and designs are often made up of very fine lines. Prints may be made from flat wood blocks (woodcuts), from metal plates (etchings and engravings), from specially prepared stone (lithographs), from silk stretched over a frame (silk-screen prints), or by photography. These different forms of graphic art all make it possible for the artist to produce many copies of a drawing.

▼ *A Japanese graphic artist mixing colors to apply to a woodblock.*

■ LEARN BY DOING

To make a *potato print*, cut a potato in half. Use a paring knife to cut a shape from each half. Paint the flat shape with tempera paints. Press the painted side against a sheet of white or colored paper. Repeat the printing to obtain an overall design, or use several shapes to make up the figure of an animal. Different colored paints may be used.

You may also carve a design into the flat side of the potato half and print in the same way. Only the raised areas of the design will show up.

To make a *cardboard print*, cut shapes from one piece of cardboard. Use white glue to attach the shapes to another piece of cardboard. Leave a space between each shape. Paint the shapes quickly with tempera. Place a piece of paper over the painted shapes and rub the paper with the bowl of a spoon. You may also use a small hand roller and water-soluble printing inks, available from any art store.

To make a *string print*, cut a piece of cardboard from the side of a cardboard box. Make a drawing with a felt-tip pen. Squeeze lines of white glue over the pen lines. Place heavy yarn over the glue and push it against the cardboard. Allow to dry. Ink and print as for a cardboard print. ■

ALSO READ: BOOK; COMMERCIAL ART; DESIGN; DRAWING; ETCHING AND EN-GRAVING; GUTENBERG, JOHANNES; PRINTING.

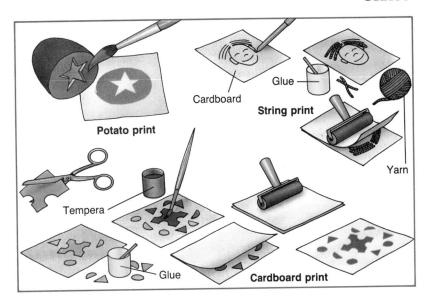

GRASS You may think of grass as the green blades that carpet a lawn or park. But there are 6,000 to 10,000 different kinds of plants belonging to the grass family. One kind, bamboo, grows as tall as a ten-story building. The stems are strong enough for house and furniture material.

The "blade"—the long, narrow leaf—is the typical structure of grass. But other plants have it, too. Cattails have bladelike leaves, but they are not grasses. The blade of corn may not appear so important to us as the ear. But corn is a grass.

The grains of corn are the seed of this grass. Grains produced by grasses—the cereal grains, like corn, wheat, oats, and rice—make grasses important as both people's and animals' food. In fact, grass is necessary to all animal life. Grain cultivation was probably what made it possible for people to begin to live in one place and build communities. Other food grasses for human beings are the shoots (young, small, soft stems) of bamboo and sugarcane.

Grass grows from the base—not the tip as do many other plants. Animals can graze on the ends of grass blades constantly, and the plant will still keep growing. As a young plant, grass puts down just one primary root. Later, more roots grow from the stem. The roots anchor grasses firmly. In dry areas, roots extend more and more—as far as ten feet (3 m) from the plant—to find water. Also, since the plant does not depend on just one stem and root system, it can survive if injured.

The numerous roots and the way the stems grow make grass one of the most useful earth-holders to prevent erosion. The destruction of grass by animals such as goats—who chew all the way down through the growing

▲ Figures, *a lithograph made by the Swiss artist Paul Klee.*

▲ *Bamboo, a giant grass that grows mostly in warm climates. The hollow woody stems are used in making various articles such as fishing rods and furniture.*

▼ *Some common grasses. From left to right: Crested dog's-tail, Common quaking grass, Common foxtail, Rough meadow grass.*

point—led to the washing away of soil and the destruction of trees in places like the Middle East. Earth has been added to long stretches of coastlines by some grasses. Their stems and blades catch sand washed into the grass by the tides.

Grass has flowers, but not pretty ones. They have no true petals—only the stamens (male organs) and pistils (female organs) necessary to reproduce.

Grasses have developed special traits for certain surroundings. Short, stubby blades and long roots grow in dry areas, for example. Scientists try, too, by crossbreeding, to develop widely different traits in cereal and turf (lawn) grasses. New turf grasses can survive in spite of bad weather. There are varieties that grow thickly, thus preserving the soil. Others form soft, luxuriant lawns that do not need to be cut often. Scientists have developed both turf and cereal grasses now that resist disease and insects far better than their wild ancestors.

ALSO READ: BOTANY; BURBANK, LUTHER; CORN; GRAIN; LEAF; PLANT BREEDING.

GRASSHOPPER The grasshopper belongs to an insect group that includes the crickets and katydids. Grasshoppers are closely related to the cockroach and praying mantis. All members of the grasshopper family (over 5,000 species) have certain characteristics. They all have unusually strong hind legs that enable them to jump long distances. These legs are often three times as long as the rest of the body. They also have two sets of large wings. The front wings are generally used as protection for the delicate rear wings, which the grasshopper uses for flying. They can fly rapidly over short distances. The species with longer wings can fly farther than the short-winged varieties. Grasshoppers also have strong jaws.

You may have heard grasshoppers make chirping sounds like those produced by crickets. Male grasshoppers "sing" in this way to attract females. Some species make these sounds by rubbing the two front wings together. Others rub the rough edge of one leg against a wing.

When young grasshoppers hatch from the egg, they look exactly like adults except that they are much smaller and have no wings. For the next six weeks, the grasshopper *molts* (sheds its hard outer shell and grows a new one) five times as it grows. After the fifth molt, the wings begin to grow. Adults range from one to five inches (2–13 cm) in length.

Grasshoppers can be found in all different colors and markings. They often look exactly like the vegetation on which they feed. Some species change color as the season changes. This protective coloration allows them to blend into their background, making them nearly invisible to their enemies.

The grasshopper will usually hop or fly away when it is threatened. But it can also produce a bitter, foul-smelling brown juice from its mouth. The juice is harmless, but it quickly discourages any attacker.

The grasshopper has been the farmer's enemy for thousands of years. Some long-winged species, *lo-*

▼ *Grasshoppers "sing" by rubbing their hind legs against their front wings. Grasshoppers are related to crickets.*

custs, migrate (travel to other places) in huge swarms (groups). Some other species occasionally produce a longer-winged generation that migrates. A swarm of locusts or other grasshoppers can make the sky appear black as far as the eye can see. When they land, they eat all the vegetation in their path. The crops of an entire state can be destroyed. (They also eat drapes and upholstery!)

Scientists and farmers are always searching for ways to destroy these pests. Many primitive peoples try to make up for the loss of their crops by eating the locusts. (They dry and grind the locusts before eating them.) In some parts of the world, people eat other species of grasshoppers and consider them a great delicacy.

ALSO READ: INSECT, INSECT PEST, METAMORPHOSIS, MOLTING, PROTECTIVE COLORING.

GRASSLANDS see PRAIRIE.

GRAVITY AND GRAVITATION

In the 1660's a young British scientist named Isaac Newton tried to work out why the moon stayed in orbit around the Earth. Suddenly he realized the answer. (It is said that he was inspired by seeing an apple fall.) Gravity, the same force that holds you down to the Earth, reaches out into space. If the Earth had no gravity, the moon would fly off into distant space. But because of the Earth's gravity, the moon stays in orbit.

■ LEARN BY DOING

You can see how this works. Tie a ball to a piece of string. Swing the ball around your head. (Go outside to do this!) Imagine you are the Earth and the ball is the moon. You can feel the ball trying to "escape from orbit." But because you are pulling the string, it cannot. Your pull on the string is like the Earth's gravity pulling the moon. ■

Newton began to study this force, called *gravitation*. (Gravity is really the force between the Earth and objects on or near it. But the word "gravity" is now normally used to mean gravitation, too.) Newton's work unlocked one of nature's most important secrets. Other scientists, such as Galileo, had studied gravitation. Galileo showed that light objects fall as fast as heavy ones. But he did not know that the force of gravity reaches across the gulf of space. Newton used mathematics to show this was true, and to show why the moon stays in its orbit.

Gravity is the force that makes order in the universe. Without gravity, everything would float away in different directions. All objects—even an atom!—have gravity. The strength

▲ *The female of the migratory locust, a type of grasshopper.*

▼ *A powerful cannon fires a ball that eventually, because of gravity, falls to the ground (1). If the power of the cannon is increased, the rate at which the ball falls to the ground is equal to the rate at which the surface curves away from it, so the ball goes into orbit around the Earth (2). If fired at an even greater speed, the ball escapes into space (3).*

1

2

3

Planet	Weight lb (kg)	
Earth	60	(27.2)
Mercury	22.8	(10.3)
Venus	52.8	(23.9)
Mars	23.4	(10.6)
Jupiter	160	(72.6)
Saturn	53	(24)
Uranus	63	(28.6)
Neptune	67	(30.4)

If you weigh 60 pounds on Earth, how much would you weigh on the other planets? Each planet's gravity determines what you would weigh.

(The surface gravity of Pluto is unknown. Probably you would weigh about 15 pounds [6.8 kg].)

Satellites don't have to be large moons or spaceships. Somewhere in space there is a camera lost by the U.S. astronaut Michael Collins during an orbital spaceflight. It will go on orbiting the Earth for a very long time.

of an object's gravity depends on the object's *mass* (its "heaviness"). More mass means stronger gravity. Earth has more gravity than the moon. The sun has more gravity than the Earth.

Gravity's strength also depends on distance. You weigh very slightly less on a mountaintop than you do in a valley, because you are slightly farther away from the Earth's center, which is also its *center of gravity*. The lessening of gravity's pull through increasing distance is interesting. The pull lessens according to the *inverse-square law*. You are nearly 4,000 miles (6,400 km) from the Earth's center. If you went in a spaceship so that you were 4,000 miles (6,400 km) away in space, you would be twice as far from the Earth's center. You would feel one-fourth of the pull. If you went 8,000 miles (12,800 km) into space (three times as far from the Earth's center), you would feel only one-ninth of the pull, and so on.

But gravity never disappears completely. An astronaut in orbit may feel weightless ("zero gravity"), but a tiny amount of gravity is keeping his or her craft in orbit.

The force of gravity on the surface of the Earth is called 1 *g*. On other planets the force of gravity is different. If you weigh 60 pounds (27.2 kg) on the Earth, on the moon you would weigh only about 10 pounds (4.5 kg). This is because the moon's gravity is only one-sixth g. But on mighty Jupiter, the biggest planet, whose gravity is about 2⅔ g, you would weigh about 160 pounds (72.6 kg)!

Gravity seems strong, but it is really very weak. Babies are not strong, but when they lift their arms they overcome gravity. But gravity never stops working, which is why it is so important in the universe.

Gravity causes objects to *accelerate* (move faster and faster) towards each other. (In a complicated way, the moon is accelerating toward the Earth as it moves in its orbit.) Near the Earth, for every second that a falling object moves, it travels 32 feet (9.8 m) faster. This is called the *acceleration due to gravity*. It too has the symbol g, because the acceleration is used as the measure of gravity.

What *is* gravity? Newton never found out. Albert Einstein, in his general theory of relativity, gave a good explanation. Imagine a rubber sheet, stretched tightly, with a heavy object on it. The object presses the sheet down. If you roll a marble across the sheet, it is "pulled" toward the object. Einstein said we should imagine objects having rather the same effect in space as the heavy weight has on the sheet.

ALSO READ: EINSTEIN, ALBERT; FORCE; GALILEO GALILEI; MATTER; MOTION; NEWTON, SIR ISAAC; ORBIT; RELATIVITY; SATELLITE; WEIGHT.

GREAT BARRIER REEF This great chain of coral reefs and small islands extends for about 1,250 miles (2,000 km) along the northeastern coast of Australia, varying from 10 to 150 miles (16–240 km) out from the mainland. It is the largest coral structure on the Earth, ranging from 10 to 90 miles (16–145 km) wide. It gets the name "barrier" because it serves as a wall against the swells of the open ocean.

If you visited the reef, you would see coral of many shapes and colors—pink, white, purple, yellow, and gray. It took millions of years for the tiny skeletons of coral to pile up and form the reef. It covers some 80,000 square miles (207,000 sq. km), most of it under water. Many kinds of plants and animals, such as oysters, sea cucumbers, starfish, and marine snails, inhabit this reef and the surrounding waters.

Recently, the crown-of-thorns starfish that live on the reef have increased greatly in number. Scientists believe this may have occurred because their natural enemy, the triton

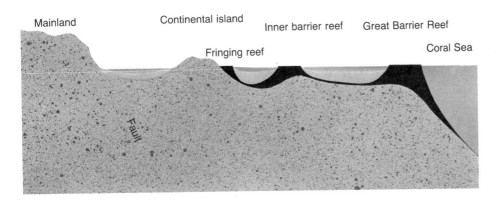

Mainland · Continental island · Inner barrier reef · Great Barrier Reef · Fringing reef · Coral Sea · Fault

◄ *The Great Barrier Reef off the coast of Australia may have been formed when a section of the coast sank downward along a fault. As the land sank, coral gradually built up islands and reefs.*

snails, have been taken away by tourists. (Many people like to collect the shells of these snails.) The starfish have been eating the live corals, destroying large areas of coral, which is then not replaced when the sea washes it away. Scientists have tried importing enemies of the starfish, such as a tiny shrimp. Divers have also killed the starfish by hand with injections. But no satisfactory way has yet been found to protect the Great Barrier Reef.

ALSO READ: CORAL.

GREAT BRITAIN see BRITISH ISLES.

GREAT LAKES
Lake Superior, Lake Huron, Lake Michigan, Lake Erie, and Lake Ontario make up the Great Lakes, the largest group of freshwater lakes in the world. The five Great Lakes combined cover an area almost the size of Oregon. Lake Superior is the largest freshwater lake in the world in terms of area. (Lake Baikal, in the Soviet Union, is the largest freshwater lake in terms of volume.) The smallest of the Great Lakes, Lake Ontario, is about the size of New Jersey. All of the lakes except Lake Michigan, which lies entirely in the United States, are shared by the United States and Canada and form part of the border between these countries.

The Great Lakes were formed 10,000 or more years ago, during the last ice age. At that time, the Earth's northern icecap reached far down into North America. As the glaciers (huge sheets of ice) moved, they scratched deep holes into the Earth, and the weight of the ice caused the land surface to sink. When it became warmer and the ice melted, lakes were formed. The Great Lakes, like 90 percent of the world's other lakes, are the remnants of these.

No major rivers empty into the lakes. Instead, they are fed by a large number of streams and creeks. Rivers connect the lakes, and water flows through the lakes from west to east—from Superior and Michigan into Huron, from Huron into Erie, and from Erie into Ontario. From Lake Ontario, water flows through the St. Lawrence River into the Atlantic Ocean.

The water level of the Great Lakes is slowly rising, and is likely to rise further over the next few years. Experts say that the level of Lake Michigan, for example, may rise three feet (1 m) over the next ten years. If this happens, homes near the lake's edge could be in danger from flooding.

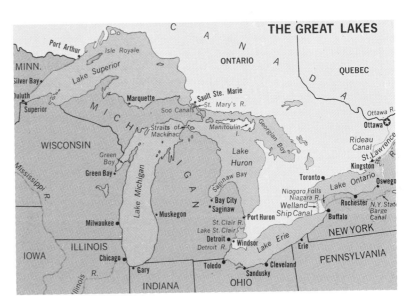

THE GREAT LAKES

▲ *The Niagara Falls on the St. Lawrence River.*

The Dust Bowl is a region in the Great Plains where rain and wind eroded the rich soil because people used poor farming methods. During the 1930's, the soil vanished in terrible dust storms, causing many people to flee their farms.

A Water Highway The Great Lakes are deep and wide. But the rivers that join the lakes to one another are shallow, and in places are broken by steep rapids and waterfalls. The Niagara River, which links Lake Erie and Lake Ontario, is broken by Niagara Falls, where water tumbles down about 160 feet (49 m). Therefore, the natural waterways that connect the lakes are of little use to ships. For a long time, the lakes were landlocked. A ship could be built on Lake Ontario, for example, and it could sail back and forth on that lake. But it could not sail up the Niagara River to Lake Erie or down the St. Lawrence River to the Atlantic.

All this has changed. Shallow rivers have been deepened. Canals have been dug to bypass the rapids. Oceangoing ships now steam up the St. Lawrence River, through the St. Lawrence Seaway, and through all the Great Lakes. Oceangoing ships can now reach 2,000 miles (3,200 km) into North America.

Two other canal systems have been dug. They provide "back doors" into the Great Lakes for barges and other small boats. The New York State Barge Canal connects Lakes Erie and Ontario with the Hudson River, which leads to the Atlantic Ocean. The Illinois Waterway connects Lake Michigan at Chicago with the Illinois River, which leads to the Mississippi River and the Gulf of Mexico.

New Problems for the Lakes The many canals that have been built have solved the problem of how to move cargo around the Great Lakes. However, a serious problem remains—water pollution. Increased shipping on the lakes has helped to pollute the water. Cargo ships and pleasure boats release oil and gasoline into the water. Sewage and industrial wastes are carried by small rivers into the lakes. Large factories on the shores deposit all kinds of waste chemicals into the lakes. Garbage from towns and cities has also been dumped into the water. This pollution is causing great, rapid changes in the lakes. Plants and fish that were once plentiful have died out. Commercial fishing, an important Great Lakes business, has decreased. The number of beaches has grown smaller and smaller as spots where swimming was once safe and enjoyable have become polluted. Lake Erie has probably the most serious pollution problem of any of the Great Lakes. In recent years, the United States and Canada have begun programs to clean up the water of the lakes.

The water levels of the Great Lakes vary from season to season and from year to year, depending upon the amount of rain or snow that falls. With less rainfall or snowfall, harbors are not as deep as normal and cargo ships must carry smaller loads. Wind and air pressure can cause the water surface of the Great Lakes to rise and fall in different locations, sometimes creating a rhythmic change in water level, known as a *seiche*.

ALSO READ: GLACIER, ICE AGE, LAKE, NIAGARA FALLS, ST. LAWRENCE SEAWAY, WATER POLLUTION.

GREAT PLAINS That vast, almost treeless grassland called the Great Plains stretches from northern Canada to central Texas. The Plains stretch eastward from the Rocky Mountains to the Mississippi River Valley. The western part of the region is higher above sea level than the eastern part. The Rocky Mountain states of Montana and Wyoming are nearly a mile (1.6 km) above sea level. Nebraska, Kansas, and Oklahoma, on the eastern side, are one-third to one-half mile (540–800 m) above sea level.

The eastern part of the Great Plains is fairly moist, but the western part is fairly dry. Winters on the Plains are cold. Blizzards sweep across the open spaces. Summers are hot. Winds are strong.

Great herds of bison once grazed on the Great Plains. Indian tribes roamed the land, hunting the bison. Then pioneers began pushing westward across the Plains on their way to California in the mid-1800's. Cowboys followed. Railroads soon came to the West, bringing settlers bent on plowing the sod (grass-covered earth) of the Plains. These settlers were called "sodbusters." The bison began to disappear because the settlers killed many of them. The railroads and ranches began to occupy their grazing lands.

Irrigation has since improved farming in the drier parts of the Great Plains. Today, wheat and corn carpet the eastern part. Cattle and sheep graze on the western pasturelands. Problems have been caused by too much grazing in some areas of the Plains. The grass cannot grow back if the cattle or sheep eat into the base of the plant. When the grass dies, strong winds blow away the rich topsoil. Some ranchers irrigate the pastures to increase the growth of the grass. Conservationists also work to restore pasturelands.

ALSO READ: BISON; COYOTE; INDIANS, AMERICAN; PRAIRIE; PRAIRIE DOG; WESTWARD MOVEMENT; WHEAT.

GREAT SALT LAKE The Great Salt Lake in Utah is the largest inland salt lake in North America. Many thousands of years ago, during the Ice Age, a much larger, freshwater lake existed here. But conditions changed, and little fresh water flowed into the lake. Meanwhile, evaporation continued. The lake shrank. But, while water evaporated, the salts that had been dissolved in it did not. They stayed in the water, which became saltier and saltier. As a result, Great Salt Lake today is eight times saltier than the ocean.

■ **LEARN BY DOING**
Take a shallow pie pan. Fill it almost to the top with water. Sprinkle in three or four tablespoons of salt and take a taste. Now place the dish in the hot sun for a day. Look again. The water level should have dropped; some of the water has *evaporated*. Taste it again. Is it saltier than before? ■

The Great Salt Lake is so salty that few animals can live in it. Brine shrimp do exist, and two kinds of brine flies. Blue-green algae grow. But no fish live in the lake.

Want to try swimming? Floating on the lake's surface is like lying on a couch, because the heavy salt water holds up your body. But when you come out, all covered with salt crust, you will want to head for the nearest freshwater shower!

ALSO READ: BUOYANCY, DEAD SEA.

GREAT WALL OF CHINA
Imagine an immense wall, up to 30 feet (9.1 m) high in some places and sometimes 30 feet (9.1 m) wide at the base, stretching over deserts, mountains, rivers, and valleys for more than 1,500 miles (2,400 km)—the distance between Washington, D.C., and Colorado. The Great Wall of China is such a wall. Much of it can still be seen winding through northern China, from the Yellow Sea westward to the Yellow River and to the eastern edge of Tibet.

More than 2,000 years ago, the first emperor of the Ch'in dynasty wanted to protect and unite China. He had already brought the different parts of China under his rule. Wandering tribes had been invading from the north. To keep them out, the emperor decided to connect shorter walls that had previously been built by individual Chinese states. Hundreds of thousands of Chinese laborers worked to build the Great Wall, with its dou-

▲ *People don't need air mattresses or inner tubes to float on the surface of the Great Salt Lake.*

▲ *A section of the Great Wall of China winding its way across a mountain range.*

1109

▲ *A traditional Greek windmill on the holiday island of Mykonos.*

▲ *A Greek soldier, called an* evzone, *guards the Tomb of the Unknown Soldier in Athens.*

ble thickness of stones and sun-dried bricks, filled with earth to the top. Watchtowers 40 feet (12.2 m) high were spaced about 100 yards (91 m) apart. The top of the wall was wide enough to be a roadway.

Later, invaders from the north managed to break through the Great Wall. Much of the wall was rebuilt during the Ming dynasty in the 1400's and 1500's. Later Chinese rulers neglected it. Sections of the Great Wall have been rebuilt by the Chinese Communist government and are open to visitors today.

ALSO READ: CHINA.

GREECE In ancient times, Greece was the center of a brilliant and powerful civilization. Today, it is a small southeastern European nation almost the same size as the state of Alabama. Northern Greece is covered by high mountain ranges that enclose fertile valleys. The highest peak is Mount Olympus, the legendary home of ancient Greek gods. The Isthmus of Corinth lies between northern and southern Greece. The hilly southern part of the country is a peninsula called the Peloponnesus. Athens, the capital of Greece, is situated inland from the Isthmus of Corinth. The country's most important port, Piraeus, is near Athens. (See the map with the article on EUROPE.)

No part of Greece is far from the water. Two arms of the Mediterra-

nean Sea, known as the Ionian Sea and the Aegean Sea, cut deep gulfs and bays into the land. Hundreds of beautiful islands surround the mainland. The largest Greek island is Crete. The climate of Greece is similar to that of other countries bordering the Mediterranean Sea. Winters are rainy and mild. Summers are warm and dry.

About three out of every ten Greek people make their living by farming. But much of the land is poor and rocky. Only three-tenths of Greek soil can support farming. The northern provinces of Macedonia and Thessaly produce most of the grain crop. Olive trees and grapes grow on mountain slopes. Other products include tobacco and cotton. Factories turn these products into olive oil, wine, cigarettes, and cloth.

Greece has a long coastline and many sheltered bays. Fish are plentiful. Greece has been a seafaring nation since ancient times. The Greek merchant marine today is one of the largest in the world, and Greek ships carry goods to many countries.

More than 3,000 years ago the people of Greece developed the greatest early Western civilization. Many Greek words became part of other languages. Greek literature, philosophy, art, and architecture influenced other Western civilizations. The Greek Empire reached its height during the 400's B.C. Less than 300 years later, the Romans gained control of part of the Empire.

GREECE

Capital City: Athens (886,000 people).
Area: 50,944 square miles (131,944 sq. km).
Population: 10,100,000.
Government: Republic.
Natural Resources: Bauxite, chromite, lignite.
Export Products: Fruits, minerals, textiles, tobacco.
Unit of Money: Drachma.
Official Language: Greek.

The land later became part of the Byzantine Empire until the crusaders arrived in the early 1200's. Greece was ruled by the Ottoman Turks from the 1300's until 1829, when the country won its independence. A constitutional monarchy was established in 1844. Greece had a military government from 1967 to 1974, when civilian rule was restored. A republic was established in 1975. In 1981 Greece became a member of the European Economic Community.

ALSO READ: ACROPOLIS; AEGEAN SEA; ATHENS; EUROPEAN COMMUNITY; GREECE, ANCIENT; GREEK LITERATURE; MACEDONIA.

GREECE, ANCIENT For many centuries, Greece was the center of the ancient world. The Greeks did not acquire their power only through military conquests. Their greatness was largely the result of the achievements of their artists, scientists, and philosophers. Everywhere Greek traders went, they took Greek ideas with them. People throughout the ancient world were influenced by Greek thought and culture. We can still see and feel that influence.

The Beginning and the Growth
Ancient Greece covered most of the same land as modern Greece, including several islands in the Ionian and Aegean seas. It was a small, mountainous land, with beautiful blue seas and skies. Most of the people were farmers who grew olives and raised sheep. The first great civilization in the area of the Aegean Sea was on the island of Crete. This was the powerful Minoan civilization, which began around 3000 B.C. The Minoans were a peaceful and artistic people. They were also prosperous traders. The wealth and beauty of their capital city, Knossos, was widely famed. About 1450 B.C. the Mediterranean island of Thēra

(Santorini) exploded. Huge waves battered Crete. Debris from the explosion wrecked Crete's agriculture. The Minoan civilization was at an end.

The Mycenaeans, a people from mainland Greece, took over Crete. The Mycenaeans then became the major power in the Aegean area. They developed a civilization in Greece and built magnificent palaces and tombs in their chief city, Mycenae. The Mycenaeans were a warlike people, and they traveled far in search of new lands to conquer. The Trojan War was probably fought between the Mycenaeans and the city of Troy in Asia Minor (now Turkey). The Mycenaean civilization was invaded by savage tribes from the north, the Dorians, in about 1100 B.C. These invasions of Greece lasted until 750 B.C. This was a violent time of fighting, poverty, and misery for the Greek people. During these difficult years, Greeks began to form colonies in other regions.

Many Greeks sailed to islands in the Aegean Sea. Others settled along the coast of Asia Minor and called their colonies Ionia. Other Greeks founded colonies in lands around the western Mediterranean. The people who stayed in Greece built fortified cities to protect themselves. Several of these cities became so powerful that they formed their own governments and became self-ruling *city-states*. A city-state included the city itself and

▲ *The ancient Greeks richly decorated their temples and public buildings. Colorful frescoes such as this one adorned the Palace of Knossos, Crete, the capital of the great Minoan civilization.*

▲ *A marble sculpture carved during the Hellenistic Age when Greek art and science spread to Egypt and the Near East.*

1111

GREECE, ANCIENT

▶ *A bust of Pericles, the Athenian known as the "Father of Democracy."*

▼ *A Greek hoplite (infantry soldier) wearing armor, including a Corinthian helmet.*

soldiers, and all children were taught to be physically tough. The men lived in military barracks until they were 30 years old. Athens became famous as an artistic and cultural center. The architecture, drama, sculpture, and poetry produced in Athens are still admired today.

Times of War and Times of Peace
Around 560 B.C., the Greek colonies were conquered by Lydia, a neighboring kingdom. Then the powerful Persian Empire conquered Lydia and sent a series of massive armies to invade Greece. In 490 B.C., the Greeks won a great victory over the Persians at the Battle of Marathon. But another Persian army defeated the Spartans at Thermopylae and then proceeded to burn the city of Athens, which had been abandoned. The Athenians gathered their strength and destroyed the Persian fleet at the naval battle of Salamis. The Persian armies in Greece were defeated by 479 B.C. Athens then entered its most glorious era, the Age of Pericles, or "Golden Age."

Pericles (about 490–429 B.C.), the ruler of Athens, was a brilliant man and a famed *orator* (speaker). Under

the land and small villages surrounding it. Although they did not have one central government, the people of the Greek city-states had a deep national pride. At this time they called themselves *Hellenes*, and their country *Hellas*. They spoke the same language, shared the same customs, and believed in the same gods. They loved their country and felt immensely superior to the rest of the world. Many of the city-states built fleets of ships, and soon the Greeks became the most powerful traders in the Mediterranean.

The two greatest city-states were Sparta and Athens. Sparta was a military state. Its citizens led a harsh existence. All boys were trained to be

▼ *The Acropolis of Athens is now only a ruin, but 2,500 years ago it was the hub of Greek civilization.*

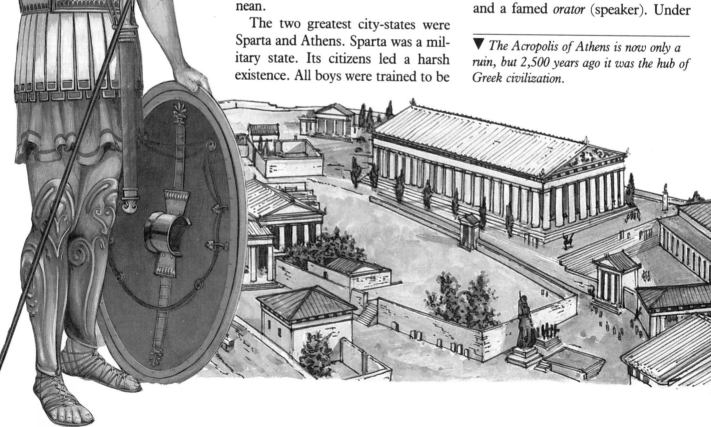

his leadership, Athens became the foremost city of the ancient world. Some of the greatest artists, writers, and philosophers of all time gathered there. Many of the most beautiful temples on the Acropolis, a mountain rising above Athens, were built. The Athenians developed a system of government known as *democracy*, which gave every free man a vote and the right to hold office. Other Greek city-states became jealous and resentful of Athens's power.

In 431 B.C., war broke out between Sparta and Athens. This was the Peloponnesian War, named for the peninsula on which Sparta was built. The other city-states chose sides, and Greece was divided. The war ended in 404 B.C. with the defeat of Athens. Much unrest followed, as the victorious city-states fought for power.

In 338 B.C. Macedonia, a country north of Greece, invaded the land. Alexander the Great of Macedonia became ruler two years later. Alexander deeply admired everything that was Greek and carried Greek ways throughout the enormous empire that he built. The two centuries following Alexander's death, in 323 B.C., are called the *Hellenistic Period*. The city-states tried to revive their former power during this time. But Greek culture had lost much of its earlier strength and beauty. The Romans conquered Greece between about 146 and 27 B.C., and made it into a Roman province. The city-states were broken up, and the history of Greece then became merged with that of the Roman Empire.

Gods, Games, and Great Men
The Greeks believed in many gods. Delphi was the holiest Greek city. Delphi had a magnificent temple dedicated to the god Apollo and a famous *oracle*, where a priestess was believed to speak Apollo's words. She would fall into a trance and make strange sounds, which the priests interpreted (explained) to the people.

The Greeks enjoyed all kinds of festivals. Their most famous were the Olympic Games. Athletes competed in discus-throwing, running, chariot-racing, and many other contests. Today's Olympic Games are loosely based on the ancient Greek games. Theater was another favorite entertainment. It was educational, too, so the wise leaders often allowed poor people to attend free. The theaters were huge outdoor arenas with seats carved out of stone.

The Greeks developed the study of many sciences, including geography, botany, zoology, and geometry. A Greek doctor, Hippocrates, is regarded as the "Father of Medicine." The great philosophers Aristotle and Plato developed principles of conduct that people still respect and try to live by today. Greek architects developed a style of architecture based on soaring columns and spacious courts. For the first time, sculptors began to portray the human body more realistically. They also sculpted beautiful, idealized human figures. The fine work of Greek painters can still be seen in museums on vases painted with graceful and lively figures.

The achievements of the ancient Greeks formed the basis of our Western civilization. The Romans copied and preserved much of Greek culture. During the period called the Renaissance, people in Europe had a renewed interest in the arts and ideas of ancient Greece. To this day, the Western world has been deeply influenced by Greek ideas in architecture, art, philosophy, and literature. The governments of many modern nations are based on the Greek ideals of democracy.

ALSO READ: ALEXANDER THE GREAT; ARISTOTLE; ATHENS; DEMOCRACY; GODS AND GODDESSES; GREECE; GREEK; GREEK ART; GREEK LITERATURE; HIPPOCRATES; HOMER; OLYMPIC GAMES; PERSIA; PHILOSOPHY; PLATO; RENAISSANCE; ROME, ANCIENT; TROJAN WAR.

▲ *Greek women usually wore a loose dress called a* chiton *in either the Dorian style* (left), *with its deep-folded top, or the Ionian style* (right), *which had no fold but was pinned or sewn along the arms and gathered at the waist by a girdle.*

▼ *A stone inscribed in ancient Greek.*

▲ *The ancient Greeks believed in athletics as a way of developing strong, healthy bodies. Wrestling was a favorite sport.*

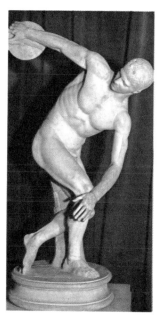

▲ *A Roman marble copy of a Greek bronze sculpture,* The Discus Thrower, *by Myron.*

GREEK Greek is one of the great roots of the tree of languages spoken in the Americas and Europe. Words taken from the ancient Greek spoken several centuries before Christ are a basic part of today's English, Spanish, French, and Italian. Greek words continue to be used in naming new inventions and discoveries in medicine and science.

Greek was originally the language of the Hellenic people who lived in regions around the Aegean Sea. Ancient Greek was a rhythmic, musical language, and much great literature was written in it. Terms coined by ancient Greek scholars in their studies of the arts and sciences were gradually picked up by other peoples in distant lands. Our words *democracy*, *philosophy*, *mathematics*, *music*, *arithmetic*, and many others come directly from Greek words. Some other English words have been created from Greek words. The word *telephone*, for example, comes from the Greek words *tele* ("far") and *phone* ("sound"). The word *alphabet* comes from the Greek letters *alpha* and *beta*, the first two letters of the Greek alphabet, written α and β in Greek.

Like all languages, Greek gradually changed over the centuries. Modern Greek is different from ancient Greek, although the same alphabet is used. Two forms of the Greek language are used in Greece today—*katharevousa*, and *demotic*. Katharevousa is based on ancient Greek. It is taught in school and used in government. Demotic is popularly used in everyday speech. A boy introducing himself in katharevousa would say: "*Kalimera*," (kah-lee-MAY-rah) (Good Morning) "*onomazome Alexandros*." (Oh-noh-MAH-zoh-me al-LAY-xahn-dros.) (My name is Alexandros.) Written, it would look like this: Καλημερα. Ονομάζομαι Ἀλέξανδρος.

ALSO READ: ALPHABET, LANGUAGES.

GREEK ART The sculpture and architecture of ancient Greece were probably greater than that of any other civilization in history. Even today artists study the sculpture done by Greek sculptors more than 2,000 years ago. Architects still design many-pillared buildings that recall Greek architecture.

Few undamaged originals of Greek sculpture and architecture survive from the days of ancient Greece. The large paintings of the Greeks have all disappeared. Much of what we know of Greek sculpture comes from copies made by the Romans of the original statues.

Minoan Art Great talent for art and the love of beauty existed in the Aegean Sea region long before the Greeks became a civilization. On the island of Crete, in the Aegean Sea south of Greece, a civilization arose more than 4,000 years ago. These early Cretans, called Minoans (after a king, Minos), built large palaces with great courtyards, big stairways, and beautiful paintings. No one knows what rulers built these palaces. An elaborate palace was erected at Knossos, the Minoan capital. There were no fortifications, so the Minoans were probably not warlike. Their art was gay and full of rhythm. They made delicate silver, gold, and bronze containers. They also made beautiful pottery. They decorated it with designs of animal life, often of creatures from the waters around the island.

Across the Aegean Sea from Crete, at about 1000 B.C., the civilization of Greece began to rise. Pottery-making was an important art in the early Greek civilization. Today, the only way we have of knowing the extraordinary Greek skill at painting is from the pottery that has survived since that time. More than 100,000 vases exist that were made by the Greeks between 800 and 100 B.C. Just imagine how many vases they must have made, if this many have lasted 2,000 to 3,000 years!

The earliest vases were often decorated in circles and squares and diamond shapes in dark brown or black on a tan clay. Certain styles, colors, and shapes were made in different parts of Greece. Later, vases were decorated with pictures. The vase painter often used stories from mythology as his theme. Certain artists became famous for their vases. After some hundreds of years of vase painting, the artists had learned how to give a three-dimensional appearance to their vase paintings, giving the feeling of depth to a flat surface.

Greek Sculpture   About the mid-600's B.C., the Greeks began carving sculpture, mostly statues of their many gods. At first their human figures looked very much like the kind of sculpture made in Egypt, with hair sculpted in even rows and almond-shaped eyes carved under rainbow-shaped eyebrows. Sculpture improved very rapidly. During the next 200 years, Greek sculptors studied the structure of the human body. They began to carve figures that showed their increasing knowledge of the muscles and bones of the human body. Many temples were being built at this time such as the beautiful one to Athena (the goddess of wisdom and the arts) at Delphi. Sculptures of gods and goddesses were placed in these temples.

The Greeks admired the human form and naturally liked to do sculptures of beautiful women and athletic men. *The Discus Thrower* is a sculpture of an athlete done about 450 B.C. by the sculptor Myron. Shown here is a Roman copy done in marble from the Greek bronze original (since lost). If you have seen a discus thrown, you will understand that the sculptor has caught the athlete in the moment just before he throws the discus. It is a short moment in time. Myron had studied the human body so well that

he made this complicated movement look easy.

The period of Greek art after the conquests of Alexander the Great is called the *Hellenistic Period* (323 to 27 B.C.). At this time there was less interest in portraying gods and goddesses, and more interest in sculpture that portrayed ordinary people. The statue shown here is of a little girl with a dove, the kind of scene that appealed to the Hellenistic sculptors. Other popular subjects were old fishermen, market women, and sleeping children. A statue has even been found of a jockey on a horse.

In the past 200 years, thanks to the science of archeology, much of Greece's ancient art has been found and studied. Nearly every year brings a new discovery.

ALSO READ: ACROPOLIS; GODS AND GODDESSES; GREECE, ANCIENT; SCULPTURE.

GREEK GOD   see GODS AND GODDESSES; GREECE, ANCIENT.

GREEK LITERATURE   Almost all the different forms of European literature began in ancient Greece—such forms as epic and lyric poetry, biographies, histories, essays, speeches, plays and novels. The earliest kinds of Greek literature were folk tales and songs. Two of the greatest works of Greek literature, the epic poems the *Iliad* and the *Odyssey*, were probably told by the poet Homer before 800 B.C. The *epic* is a very long poem that tells a story in flowing, majestic language. The *Iliad* tells about the Trojan War and the destruction of Troy. The *Odyssey* is a story about the travels of the Greek hero Ulysses after the fall of Troy. Another master of epic poetry was Hesiod, who wrote *Works and Days*, the daily life of a farmer. The Greeks developed *lyric* poetry, too. Origi-

▲ *A Hellenistic Greek sculpture shows a girl protecting her pet dove from a snake.*

▲ *A gold jug, dating from 1500 B.C., in the shape of a lion's head. It was used at Mycenae for pouring offerings of wine to the gods.*

1115

▲ *Three famous Greek dramatists. Sophocles and Euripides wrote tragedies in ancient Greece's "Golden Age." Aristophanes (448–380 B.C.) wrote comedies. From Athens, the love of drama spread throughout the Greek world.*

▲ *Horace Greeley, U.S. journalist of the 1800's.*

nally, a lyric was a song accompanied by a musical instrument called a lyre. Pindar was possibly the greatest lyric poet. A woman named Sappho wrote beautiful love poems in this style.

The so-called "Golden Age" of Greece (about 480–323 B.C.) was the most outstanding period of Greek literature. Athens was then the cultural center of Greece, and this time is sometimes called the *Attic* Period (referring to Athens). Three brilliant playwrights, Aeschylus, Sophocles, and Euripides, created plays with sad endings called *tragedies*. Another playwright, Aristophanes, wrote *comedies*, which mocked the leaders of the time. Their works are still performed. Herodotus wrote histories of the Greek and Persian wars and described his travels to faraway places. Plato and Aristotle wrote about philosophy.

During the Hellenistic Period (323 to 27 B.C.), Greek writers looked mainly to the past and developed few new ideas. But after Greece became part of the Roman Empire, several great writers appeared. Plutarch wrote *Parallel Lives*, biographies of renowned Greeks and Romans. Among many important scientific books were those by the geographer Ptolemy and the physician Galen.

ALSO READ: AESCHYLUS; ARISTOTLE; DRAMA; GREECE, ANCIENT; HOMER; PHILOSOPHY; PLATO; PLUTARCH; POETRY.

GREELEY, HORACE (1811–1872)

The famous words of advice "Go West, young man, go West!" were said by Horace Greeley, a U.S. editor and journalist. Greeley was strongly in favor of the settlement of the Western frontier. He had strong opinions about many other issues.

Horace Greeley was born in Amherst, New Hampshire. He left school at 14 to become a printer's apprentice (trainee). At age 20 he went to New York City and soon became editor of a weekly literary magazine, the *New Yorker*. Later, he edited the *Jeffersonian* and the *Log Cabin*, both weekly campaign literature of the Whig Party. In 1841, Greeley founded the *New York Tribune* and was its editor for the next 30 years. It sold for one cent and was called a "penny paper."

Greeley was able to influence many people through his newspaper. He wrote articles urging unrestricted voting rights for everyone, emigration to the West, and educational reform. He opposed slavery and helped found the Republican Party, which was formed mainly as an anti-slavery party. After the Civil War, Greeley was against any harsh treatment of the defeated South.

In 1870, Greeley sponsored a group that settled in Colorado. The settlement later became the city of Greeley. Horace Greeley always wanted to hold a political office, and he ran unsuccessfully several times. In 1872, he ran for the office of President as a Liberal Republican. Although he was also supported by the Democrats, Greeley was defeated by the Republican candidate, Ulysses S. Grant.

ALSO READ: JOURNALISM, WESTWARD MOVEMENT.

GREENHOUSE

Flowers, fruits, and vegetables bloom in the light and warmth of the sun and drink the water in the air. But what happens at night or in the winter? What happens in dry climates? Many flowers, fruits, and vegetables would not be available in many parts of the world for most of the year if not for greenhouses.

A greenhouse is a glass-enclosed building in which plants, fruits, or vegetables are grown in an artificial (man-made) environment. In a greenhouse, we are able to recreate the conditions (light, temperature, and humidity) that occur in any season anywhere in the world. Greenhouses are used also to protect delicate plants until they are large enough to be planted outdoors.

The main source of light and heat in a greenhouse is the sun. The glass panes of the walls and ceiling are placed at the best angle to receive the sun's rays. Artificial lighting is often used also, depending on the region, season, and natural weather conditions. Imagine how fast some plants can grow when they are exposed to 24 hours of "sunlight" every day! Sometimes too much sunlight is harmful to a delicate plant, so the walls of the greenhouse are painted to block out the sun's rays. The entering rays of light are a form of energy that passes easily through glass. After the rays are absorbed by the plants, the energy changes—from light to heat. This heat energy cannot pass back through the glass very easily, so most remains inside.

The *humidity* (moisture in the air) is controlled by the amount of water used in the greenhouse. The soil may be watered sparsely or thoroughly saturated—depending on the natural climate where the plant normally grows. Sometimes the floor of the greenhouse is watered, so that when the water evaporates there will be more moisture in the air.

Most greenhouses are equipped with heaters. They also have ventilators, or openings, in the roof to take advantage of any helpful weather conditions. The atmosphere in a greenhouse can be made to resemble a small tropical jungle (*hothouse*) or a hot, dry desert (*dry stove*). A *conservatory* is usually used only for rare plants.

The Earth's atmosphere is rather like an enormous greenhouse. When the sun's rays are "trapped," we call this the *greenhouse effect*. The planet Venus is much closer to the sun than the Earth is, and has a much thicker atmosphere. The light energy from the sun enters Venus's atmosphere, and very little of it can escape. There is what we call a *runaway greenhouse effect*. If it were not for the greenhouse effect, the surface of Venus would have temperatures a little more than twice those on the Earth. In fact, surface temperatures on Venus are about 900° F (480° C)! Scientists worry that the fumes we put into our own atmosphere may create a runaway greenhouse effect on Earth.

ALSO READ: BOTANICAL GARDEN, CLIMATE, PHOTOSYNTHESIS.

GREENLAND The largest island in the world is Greenland, lying off the northeast coast of Canada in the North Atlantic Ocean. It is three times the size of Texas. Greenland belongs to Denmark, which established home rule on the island in 1979. Greenlandic place names came into use with Greenland called Kalâtdlit-Nunât. (See the map with the article on NORTH AMERICA.)

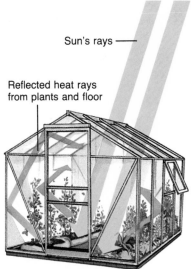

▲ *The inside of a greenhouse becomes warm because heat rays from the sun can come in through the glass, in the form of light, but have difficulty escaping once their energy has been reduced by contact with the plants and floor.*

GREENLAND

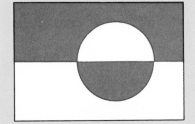

Capital City: Godthaab (Nûk) (7,200 people).
Area: 839,999 square miles (2,175,587 sq. km).
Population: 50,000 people.
Government: Home rule legislature granted by Denmark in 1979.
Natural Resources: Cryolite.
Export Products: Fish and fish products, lignite (brown coal).
Unit of Money: Krone.
Languages: Danish, Greenlandic, Eskimo languages.

▲ *A fishing village on Davis Strait, on the southwestern coast of Greenland. The strait separates Greenland from Baffin Island, in Canada.*

The icecap that covers much of the island reaches a thickness of over two miles (3.2 km). It has pressed down the land beneath it, lowering its elevation. The coast of Greenland is jagged and rocky, with many small islands offshore. Great glaciers make their way down to the sea.

The first European settlers on the island called it "Greenland" to attract more people to join them. But very little greenery grows there. The summer is short, and even in July the temperature in Godthaab (Nûk), the capital, averages 50° F (10° C).

The few people who live in Greenland have settled mainly along the west coast—the only area free of ice. Most of the people are of mixed descent—Eskimo, Danish, and Norwegian. Their main occupations are codfishing and hunting for seals. Most of the cod is exported. Some Greenlanders still depend on the seal for meat, fuel, and clothing. The people in modern settlements in the southwest also grow vegetables and raise sheep.

ALSO READ: DENMARK, GLACIER.

GREENWICH TIME   see TIME.

GREETING CARD   Many people enjoy sending and receiving greeting cards for a birthday, Valentine's Day, Christmas, or other important days.

The custom is very old. The first printed valentine cards were made in England in the 1600's, and the first Christmas card was made in London in 1843. Birthday cards soon became popular, too.

Today, you can buy greeting cards for many other occasions, including Thanksgiving, Halloween, Mother's Day, and Father's Day. Special cards can be sent to friends who are graduating from school, getting married, having an anniversary, or leaving on a trip, wishing them good luck. Other cards welcome a new baby, thank someone for a gift, or express the hope that someone who is sick will be better soon. There are even funny cards for no particular occasion at all.

The earliest greeting cards were printed on a single piece of paper. Today's card is usually folded in half. It may have a beautiful picture or brightly colored design on the front and a thoughtful or amusing message inside.

Until early in this century, most greeting cards were homemade, and homemade cards are still often the best. They can mean more to those who receive them than store-bought ones. You can make designs or pictures for a card by painting, drawing, or pasting shapes cut from colored paper. Try making up a short poem for the message.

GRENADA   see WEST INDIES.

▼ *Three old greeting cards, commemorating St. Valentine's Day, the Fourth of July, and Christmas.*

GRIFFITH, D. W.

GREY, LADY JANE (1537–1554)
Lady Jane Grey was a great-grand-daughter of King Henry VII of England. Her parents were very strict with her and she had a very unhappy childhood. She was very studious. When she was still quite young, she could read and speak Latin, Greek, French, and Italian, as well as English.

At this time, the king of England was a young boy, Edward VI. Edward was the son of Henry VIII. He was sickly. His chief councilor was the Duke of Northumberland. The duke was the most powerful man in England after the king. The duke knew that Edward was ill and would not live very long. The duke arranged a marriage between his son, Lord Guilford Dudley, and Lady Jane Grey. The duke then had Edward sign a paper declaring that Lady Jane Grey was to be queen after he died. The duke did all this to make sure he would still stay in power after Edward's death.

Edward did die soon after the marriage. The Duke of Northumberland then declared that Lady Jane Grey was queen, but the people did not agree. They wanted Mary, Edward's half sister, to be queen. Mary was crowned queen of England instead of Lady Jane Grey. Mary then had the Duke of Northumberland, his son, and Lady Jane Grey imprisoned. Mary later ordered them beheaded. Lady Jane Grey was only 16 years old when she died.

ALSO READ: EDWARD, KINGS OF ENGLAND; HENRY, KINGS OF ENGLAND; MARY, QUEENS OF ENGLAND.

GRIEG, EDVARD (1843–1907)
The Norwegian composer, Edvard Hagerup Grieg, wrote music that expressed the spirit of his people and his country. He won lasting fame and affection for his *Concerto for Piano and Orchestra in A Minor,* his background music for the play *Peer Gynt* (written by fellow Norwegian Henrik Ibsen), and for his many songs and short piano pieces. *Songs of Norway* is based on Grieg's music.

Grieg was born in Bergen, Norway. His mother taught him to play the piano and introduced him to many folk songs and dances of his homeland. He was sent to study music in Germany at age 15, and he began to compose music there. Grieg's music took on more and more of the spirit of his country after he returned to Norway five years later. He used folk-song melodies sometimes, but more often his tunes were original. The best-known pieces of Grieg's music for *Peer Gynt* are "Morning," "Anitra's Dance," "In the Hall of the Mountain King," and "Ase's Death."

ALSO READ: COMPOSER; IBSEN, HENRIK; NORWAY.

GRIFFITH, D. W. (1875–1948)
David Wark Griffith was born in La Grange, Kentucky, and attended the University of Kentucky. He acted in plays for a company that moved from town to town. Then he went to work for the Biograph Company as a movie actor. Later, Griffith directed movies for the company. He started producing and directing movies on his own in 1913. His film about the Civil War, called *Birth of a Nation,* brought him worldwide fame. It is still shown today even though it is a "silent movie"—made before sound for movies was invented.

Griffith developed many techniques for making movies that are still used today. He started the United Artists Corporation to produce movies in 1919. His partners were three famous silent-movie stars—Charlie Chaplin, Douglas Fairbanks, and Mary Pickford. Griffith directed many silent movies for the company,

▲ *Lady Jane Grey, who was Queen of England for a few days in July 1553.*

▲ *Edvard Grieg, Norwegian composer.*

▲ *David W. Griffith, U.S. movie director.*

▲ *The brothers Wilhelm and Jakob Grimm, German collectors of fairy tales.*

February 2 is Groundhog Day. On this day the groundhog is thought to come out of hibernation and look around. Some people believe that if it sees its shadow, it goes back to sleep and winter lasts another six weeks.

▼ *A young prairie groundhog at the entrance to its burrow.*

including *Intolerance, Broken Blossoms, Way Down East,* and *Orphans of the Storm.* Griffith's contributions to the art of film-making made him one of the greatest pioneers of the motion-picture industry.

ALSO READ: CHAPLIN, CHARLIE; MOTION PICTURES.

GRIMM BROTHERS Many of our most familiar and best loved fairy tales were first written down by two brothers, Jakob Grimm (1785–1863) and Wilhelm Grimm (1786–1859). Most of the tales they collected had been passed down by word of mouth from generation to generation for hundreds of years.

The Grimm brothers were born in Hanau, Germany. The two brothers were devoted to each other and spent most of their lives working together. They both studied law at the University of Marburg. They first became interested in old languages, legends, and folk tales while they were students there. They began a lifelong study of these subjects. Both brothers worked as librarians and later as university professors. They traveled throughout Germany collecting folk tales. They listened to the old stories on farms, in the fields, everywhere they could find someone who remembered and could tell them. They also studied old manuscripts and books, searching for folk stories.

The Grimm brothers published a number of scholarly books about German language and literature. But their most famous work is a collection of German folk tales nowadays called *Grimm's Fairy Tales.* It was first published in three volumes between 1812 and 1815. Included are the famous stories "Hansel and Gretel," "Rapunzel," "Rumpelstiltskin," "Little Red Riding Hood," "Sleeping Beauty," and "Cinderella." Another well-known tale, "Snow White and the Seven Dwarfs," was chosen by Walt

Disney to be made into the first full-length animated cartoon.

ALSO READ: FAIRY TALE, FOLKLORE.

GROUNDHOG A groundhog looks like a beaver with thick, brownish-gray hair. Its stocky body is one or two feet (30–60 cm) long, with a long tail and short legs. It is a rodent related to the prairie dog and is common in eastern and northern North America. Groundhogs are also called *woodchucks* or *marmots.*

Groundhogs eat all summer. They like roots of trees, grain, and leaves, and they destroy some crops. They dig tunnels in the ground, sometimes ruining lawns. They fight stubbornly and well if attacked. You wouldn't expect them to be so fierce, if you saw them lying in the sun. They live in underground burrows in open fields or woods. You sometimes see them sitting up on their hind legs, looking for any approaching danger.

By October, a groundhog is so fat it can hardly walk. It is then ready to hibernate. It curls up in its tunnel for the winter. For about six months, the groundhog is in a very deep sleep, living off its stored fat. In spring, it wakes from its winter sleep, and then begins eating again. It usually lives from 13 to 16 years.

ALSO READ: HIBERNATION, PRAIRIE DOG, RODENT.

GROUND SQUIRREL No matter where you live in North America, you can see some variety of ground squirrel. In the West and Midwest there are gophers and prairie dogs, and in the East, chipmunks. Groundhogs (woodchucks) are another kind of ground squirrel.

Ground squirrels live in burrows, instead of in the trees like other squirrels. They eat seeds, nuts, and grain. Some hoard food in their burrows for

▲ *A ground squirrel. It is hard to tell the difference between a ground squirrel and a tree squirrel.*

winter eating. Others hibernate in their burrows.

Prairie dogs, unlike many ground squirrels, live together in big burrows on the Western prairies. They stay close to home, standing on top of little mounds containing the entrance to their burrow. Often they even stand in the burrow, with only their heads showing.

Chipmunks are less heavy-bodied and more active than many ground squirrels. They hide nuts everywhere and then forget where they put most of them. In this way they help plant many trees and bushes.

There are 33 kinds of ground squirrels in the United States, and many varieties in Africa. They vary in size—the groundhog is probably the largest U.S. variety. Most ground squirrels live alone in their burrows except when they mate. Litters contain up to ten babies.

ALSO READ: GOPHER, GROUNDHOG, PRAIRIE DOG, RODENT, SQUIRREL.

GROWTH Why aren't all people who are the same age also the same size? Any increase in the size of a living thing (or some nonliving things) is called growth. But each individual thing grows at its own rate. Not only does the rate of growth vary between individuals, but it also varies between parts of a single individual.

What is Growth? Growth in size among living things is caused by cell division. Every cell in your body is growing and dividing. Each new cell divides, in turn, into more cells. As the number of cells in your body increases, you grow. But although millions of cells divide each day, millions of others also die and pass out of the body as waste material. Therefore, growth takes place only when new cells are forming faster than old cells are dying. In a growing child, the new cells outnumber the dying cells.

Trees and other woody plants continue to grow all their lives; many animals, including human beings, do not. In these animals there comes a time when new cells no longer outnumber the dying cells and there is a balance between them.

WHAT CAUSES GROWTH? Many factors determine how and when you will grow. You have probably inherited many of your physical characteristics from your parents. For example, if your parents are taller than most other people their age, you will most likely be tall. But this factor is determined before you are born. Af-

Different parts of our bodies grow at different rates. A baby's head is about one-fourth of its total length when it is born. As the child grows, the other parts of the body—the trunk, arms, and legs—increase in size much more quickly than the head does. So, in an adult, the head is only about one-eighth of the total body length.

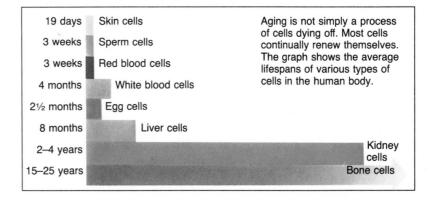

19 days	Skin cells
3 weeks	Sperm cells
3 weeks	Red blood cells
4 months	White blood cells
2½ months	Egg cells
8 months	Liver cells
2–4 years	Kidney cells
15–25 years	Bone cells

Aging is not simply a process of cells dying off. Most cells continually renew themselves. The graph shows the average lifespans of various types of cells in the human body.

The average height of U.S. children, both boys and girls, on their tenth birthday is 4 foot 6 inches (137 cm). Boys and girls on average also weigh the same at that age—69 pounds (31.3 kg).

The fastest-growing plant is the bamboo. Some species can grow at a rate of 3 feet (91 cm) in a single day. The fastest-growing animal is the blue whale. A baby whale grows to a weight of 27 tons (24.5 metric tons) in its first two years from conception. This means that it puts on more than a ton each month!

ter you are born, much of your rate of growth (or development) and eventual adult size is determined by your environment—your food, the way your body uses this food, the way you use your body. Your body is like an engine, and food is the fuel that makes it run. As your body is nourished by the food you eat, the cells grow and increase. This is why a well-balanced diet is important for a growing child.

Another factor in growth is rest and sleep. If your body does not have enough rest, it might just get too tired to "work." Exercise is the important factor in muscle growth. You have probably seen people who have developed very large muscles through exercise. And muscle development is important for both boys and girls, since muscles control even the slightest movement of the body.

How Do We Grow? You will probably be surprised to learn that you grew faster in the first two years of your life than you ever will again! From birth to adolescence (or the teens), most of your growth takes place in the "long bones"—in the arms and legs. At the end of a long bone is an "extra" piece—the *epiphysis*—joined to the main bone by softer tissue (*cartilage*). This is the only part of the bone that grows. As the epiphysis grows, the cartilage becomes absorbed in the bone, increasing the length of the entire bone. During adolescence, growth rate is again increased. Now many of your glands are influencing your body. The pituitary gland controls all your other glands, and it has been doing so all your life. At the start of adolescence, the sex glands begin to change boys into men and girls into women.

RATE OF GROWTH. Every individual grows at a different rate. In childhood, boys seem to grow faster than girls. At adolescence girls usually shoot ahead of boys in growth. At this time many girls might feel tall and

awkward. Boys might feel "puny" and worry that they will never get any taller. But by the late teens, boys not only catch up to girls, but they usually grow taller.

Sometimes certain parts of the body grow faster than others. All of a sudden the ears or feet might seem to be bigger, but the face or legs haven't changed! But the rest of the body soon catches up.

HOW TALL WILL YOU BE? Since there are so many factors that affect growth, it is impossible to predict a living thing's eventual size. For example, Asians are generally smaller than North Americans. But studies have shown that the children of Asians who have immigrated to North America grow much taller than their parents. Doctors believe that the difference in height is due to the better diet of the children.

Sometimes improper functioning of the glands will cause tremendous changes in an individual's growth and size. An overactive pituitary gland can cause such tremendous growth that the individual is considered a giant. An underactive pituitary can produce a dwarf.

■ LEARN BY DOING

Although children of the same age are all about the same height, there is quite a lot of variation.

Try making a chart of your friends' heights to find out the range of heights for your age group. Draw a vertical line and a horizontal line meeting at right angles to each other. Mark off the vertical line to represent the number of children of each height. Mark off the horizontal line to represent height in inches (or millimeters).

Get as many heights as you can for your age and fill in each block formed with a different color. You could do a similar chart for your friends' weight or shoe size. ■

ALSO READ: BONE, CELL, GENETICS, GLAND, HORMONE, HUMAN BODY.